Ethics in Educational
Leadership Programs

Ethics in Educational Leadership Programs

An Expanding Role

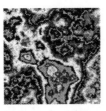

Lynn G. Beck
Joseph Murphy

CORWIN PRESS, INC.
A Sage Publications Company
Thousand Oaks, California

in collaboration with
The University Council for Educational Administration

For information address:

Corwin Press, Inc.
A Sage Publications Company
2455 Teller Road
Thousand Oaks, California 91320

SAGE Publications Ltd.
6 Bonhill Street
London EC2A 4PU
United Kingdom

SAGE Publications India Pvt. Ltd.
M-32 Market
Greater Kailash I
New Delhi 110 048 India

Printed in the United States of America

Library of Congress Cataloging-in-Publication Data

Beck, Lynn G.
    Ethics in educational leadership programs : an expanding role /
Lynn G. Beck, Joseph Murphy.
        p.   cm.
    Includes bibliographical references and index.
    ISBN 0-8039-6149-9. — ISBN 0-8039-6150-2 (pbk.)
    1. School administrators—Training of—United States—Moral and
ethical aspects. 2. School management and organization—United
States—Moral and ethical aspects. 3. Educational leadership—
United States—Moral and ethical aspects.   I. Murphy, Joseph,
1949– . II. Title.
LB1738.5.B43   1994
371.2′01—dc20   94-27450

This book is printed on acid-free paper that meets Environmental Protection Agency standards for recycled paper.

94 95 96 97 10 9 8 7 6 5 4 3 2 1

Corwin Press Production Editor: Marie Louise Penchoen

Contents

In memory of
Alexander Beck III
whose love helped to ground me

To
friends from the
first ten years

Foreword

The need for ethical behavior in the professions stems from public trust granted practitioners, whose work has vital consequences for those served. It is difficult to imagine a more vital societal interest than the well-being of children entrusted to teachers and administrators. Yet dialogue and deliberation on ethical behavior of school professionals could hardly be called lively. The consideration of ethical action in schools has usually been provoked by the heinous breach, rather than by a focus on positive responsibilities, behaviors and beliefs of school professionals who cradle such a delicate trust.

As our society becomes more culturally diverse, conflicting systems of thought claim to be guides for ethical action. What is legal? What is politically correct? What is sanctioned by tradition? Clearly, ethical behavior can be illegal, politically incorrect and irreverent. In this diverse world, there may be little agreement about what constitutes ethical action; however, understandings of ethical behavior cannot emerge if we continue to cast all difficult issues as dilemmas.

Professional behavior is reflective and takes into account what is known, what is believed, idiosyncratic circumstances, bias, the common good and the good of individuals. Professional behavior does not look for simplistic guides to action or absolutes. Thus the focus of this book is timely and critical, because it raises questions we need to face as a profession. It tells us where we are and posts an agenda for dialogue. There are many occupations that have codes of ethics—this does not make them professions. Professions are occupations in which the work is vital and complex, and this work is incapable of routinization. For the true professions, what constitutes ethical behavior is always open for review. Ethical behavior rides the emerging vistas of human possibility, generosity, and caring. Here, Professors Beck and Murphy vividly outline those vistas for our consideration. The UCEA is proud to collaborate with them in bringing this discussion to the forefront.

Patrick B. Forsyth, Executive Director
UCEA

Foreword

There is virtually universal agreement about the critical place of values and ethics in educational administration. However, agreement that something is critically important is only a starting point, an opportunity for assessment and possible action. Just how values and ethics should be reflected in scholarship and in programs for the preparation of practitioners is a pressing issue that merits serious attention. As is common in matters of importance, there are many questions and few sure answers.

To cite just a few questions in the preparation category, What should be the purpose of ethics education for administrators? Should there be a specific course or courses on ethics or should the exploration of moral issues be integrated in a variety of preparatory courses and activities? If the former, What should make up the course content? There are many possibilities: ethical positions in history of philosophy; moral dilemmas as found in histories, novels and plays; ethical dimensions to current debates on social issues; and case studies requiring choices on desirable future directions or among competing value alternatives, to mention a few. If the latter, What forms would integration take and how would it be assured?

Those who are concerned about such questions and with the larger issues of ethics as a field of inquiry will be heartened by this book by Lynn Beck and Joseph Murphy. The core of the book is found in the chapters detailing the results of a study of ethics in the administrator preparation programs of UCEA member universities. Based on surveys returned from 42 institutions, we are given a picture of what is being done and the rationales underlying the various approaches taken. These kinds of particulars will be especially interesting and useful to those planning new courses or activities on ethics in their preparation programs.

The book is rounded out by chapters on selected ways of approaching ethics, a brief look at some work on ethics in educational administration, some speculations on why moral issues are becoming more salient in writing and preparation, and a proposal that future dialogue on ethics not get bogged down in preoccupation with details. Beck and

Murphy cogently argue that the emphasis should be on the larger issues of teaching and learning, as well as the broad philosophical context of ethical thought, for instance, its relation to conceptions of knowledge, and the particulars of the human condition. Thoughtful afterwords are provided by William Foster and Robert Starratt. Foster reminds us that daily moral problems thrust upon administrators should not be allowed to overwhelm activities intended to build more desirable futures for organizations and those they serve. Starratt notes that many ethical problems have no easy solution and urges that research be undertaken to gain a better understanding of the personal struggles of those who must make difficult moral choices.

This latter suggestion serves to highlight the lack of descriptive research on values in educational administration. Even modest lines of inquiry along these lines are hard to find; for instance, there appear to be no contemporary counterparts to the relatively limited number of studies on the emergent and traditional values that came out of the University of Chicago in the 1950s and 1960s. This is surprising given the increased interest in values and ethics.

But it is probably explained by the dominance of exclusively normative concerns in recent years. These concerns have sometimes been accompanied by a rejection of scientific approaches that goes far beyond the question of studying about values in school settings. Indeed, science bashing has become an avocation in some circles. I believe the latter kind of thinking has the potential to become a major barrier to reflective and relevant work on values and ethics.

Most administrators and educators in general tend to be committed to improving the lot of children. They want the kids in their schools to learn and grow. They don't need academics to preach to them about utopian agendas. However, even the best of intentions do not guarantee desirable outcomes. Educators need to know how to move toward improved futures for their organizations and the people in them.

Obviously, thoughtful practitioners should be attuned to an array of human and humane ideals and virtues such as compassion, caring, tolerance, responsiblity, liberty, equity, self-sufficiency, adventure, community, and, especially in educational organizations, curiosity, reflective awareness, and knowledge. However, in real life ideals clash, and the history of efforts to articulate and, all too often, impose absolute values is a dismal one. In this realm as in others, deliberate choices are necessary.

Beyond a reflective sensitivity to ideals lies the daunting and difficult task of implementing them in concrete situations. It is here that concepts and explanations from the social sciences and from research on schools can be of genuine help to engaged educators. School administrators need to be able to make informed estimates of whether selected courses of action will actually accomplish desirable aims. Pitfalls and unintended consequences that could result in harm to individuals or particular groups need to be foreseen and headed off or mitigated. It seems clear that change directed toward improved futures is not very different from other kinds of organizational change. The same considerations apply. Relevant knowledge shared throughout the organization can be a major facilitator of improvement. I urge those who are concerned about values and ethics not to reject inquiry, but to welcome it. Reflective methods and the content of social and educational science can be the firm allies of those who struggle to create better futures.

In this connection, it seems necessary to point out that educational administration needs a more realistic conception of science than has been promulgated in recent years. Stereotypic portrayals of scientific positivists and inhumane technocrats are farfetched distortions of what science is all about. Science is, after all, a human creation and an activity that seeks to increase our understanding of the world and ourselves. As John Dewey reminds us, scientific methods are essentially free intelligences operating in the best manner available at a given time. The concepts and explanations of science are created by people, are tentative and are always subject to modification or replacement. There is no question that science can go wrong, even though there have been some remarkable successes. Science has the characteristics of other human creations. It is fallible, never final, always unfinished, and never a sure thing. Although this is the case with all of science, the social sciences are more problematic than the other special sciences, and the application of concepts and ideas to concrete social situations is chancier still. Given all of these limitations, why do I insist that reflective processes and the exploration of the empirical context are essential to wise moral choice? The answer is simple. It is that inquiry and science give us the best methods and content available, and the best hope of creating better futures.

It is sad commentary on our times and the frustrations that have attended them that so many have become disillusioned with the efforts of human beings to understand their world better using the methods of inquiry. My argument is not complicated. It is simply that, if we are to improve the human condition even in the small ways open to us, it helps a lot if we have insights into how things are likely to work.

Lynn Beck and Joseph Murphy's book about ethics in educational administration offers us another opportunity to renew and refresh thinking in our field. We need to do a better job with ethics and values in preparation programs and we need more and better sholarship on these topics. Beck and Murphy should be applauded for their contribution. I hope that it will help to stimulate activity in this crucial area. There is a great deal to be done.

Donald J. Willower
Pennsylvania State University

Preface

In the early years of this century, educational administration—both as a field of scholarly inquiry and as a profession—became enamored with the idea that "the perfect administrator would be one who could perfectly separate fact from value" (Foster, 1984, p. 105) and who, having done so, would make rational, objective decisions. In recent years, this image of the ideal, value-neutral leader has changed, and scholars and practitioners are evidencing a great deal of interest in the moral dimensions of educational leadership and in the ways that ethical commitments and beliefs do and should influence decisions, practices, strategies, and structures. The purpose of this volume is to explore this renewed interest in ethics in school administration, particularly as it is manifested in preparation programs for school leaders. We undertake that assignment by providing an in-depth analysis of the ethical dimensions of educational programs in University Council of Educational Administration (UCEA) institutions.

Prior to engaging in this investigation, we conducted an extensive examination of literature on the changing role of school site leaders (Beck & Murphy, 1993), on the evolution of administrator preparation programs (Murphy, 1992a; 1993b), and on ethical dimensions of educational leadership (Beck, 1992; 1994a). One of the articles that attracted our attention and eventually piqued our interest in conducting this study was Robin Farquhar's (1981) report on "learning opportunities concerned with ethics" (p. 195) in universities holding membership in the UCEA. In 1978, Farquhar contacted representatives from 48 universities in an effort to determine if they were dealing with ethics in their preparation programs "and if so, why, what, for whom, how, by whom, and with what results?" (p. 195). Only 18 (38%) of those contacted responded, leading the investigator to note, "One suspects that the vast majority of those who did not reply had nothing to say on the subject" (p. 195). Only 11 respondents indicated that their programs were even attempting to address ethical concerns, and of those, only 4 reported "distinct program components designed deliberately to focus on ethics" (p. 196). Farquhar's study led him to draw two major conclusions: "(1) ethics can and should be included in the formal preparation of educational administrators; (2) this is apparently not done widely or well at present" (p. 203).

As noted above and discussed more fully in Chapter 2, the years that have intervened since Farquhar's study have witnessed what seems to be a renewal of interest in the ethical dimensions of leadership. Therefore, it seemed to us that the time was ripe to investigate again the ways university-based programs were responding to administrative ethics. In a study modeled after Farquhar's, we contacted the heads of the departments of educational administration in UCEA member schools and asked them—or an appropriate designee—to respond in writing to a series of open-ended questions about the place of ethics in their programs.

Forty-two professors (84% response rate) provided us with thoughtful descriptions of curricula and programs, with rationales undergirding these programs, and with their perceptions of the impact of these efforts. After several rounds of data analysis in which, working both independently and cooperatively, we identified themes and patterns in the responses, we wrote to each institution where the respondent indicated that a course specifically concerned with ethics was offered in their program. These letters, addressed directly to professors responsible for instruction in the area of ethics, elicited seventeen syllabi and other items of information about these courses. We analyzed these with three goals in mind. First, we wanted to check the themes we had identified in our analyses of the questionnaire data to see if the syllabi confirmed or disconfirmed our conclusions. Second, we sought to understand the assumptions about the ethical dimensions of school leadership held by the professor(s) addressing this topic in their courses. We were, for example, interested in the goals and objectives for these courses and in the kinds of situations identified as posing ethical dilemmas for administrators. Finally, we desired to develop an understanding of the similarities and differences in the various approaches to this topic—a task undertaken through an examination of the readings, assignments, and experiences offered in these courses.

This book reports the results of our investigation. We open in Chapter 1 with a discussion of six ways of thinking about ethics that have informed recent discussions of moral leadership. Our attention then turns, in Chapter 2, to a historical overview of ethics in administrator preparation programs. We trace the waxing and waning of attention to ethical concerns and discuss factors that have shaped the directions of these programs. Chapters 3 and 4 contain a discussion of our findings. In Chapter 3, we present our analysis of the questionnaire data, noting themes and patterns in responses offered by representatives of 42 UCEA institutions. In Chapter 4, we discuss, in some detail, thirteen institutions whose programs offer courses explicitly devoted to ethics. Chapter 5 presents a discussion of issues that, in our view, must occupy the attention of academics and practitioners in coming years.

About the Authors

Lynn G. Beck is an assistant professor of educational administration at the University of California, Los Angeles. Her research and teaching focuses on administrative ethics, the principalship, and leadership preparation. Recent publications include *Understanding the Principalship: Metaphorical Themes 1920s to 1990s* (with Joseph Murphy, 1993) and *Reclaiming Educational Administration as a Caring Profession* (1994).

Joseph Murphy is professor and chair, Department of Educational Leadership at Vanderbilt University. His primary interest is in school improvement and the role that educational leaders can play in that process. His work also focuses on the preparation of school administrators. Recent books include: *Restructuring Schools: Capturing and Assessing the Phenomena* (1991), *The Landscape of Leadership Preparation: Reframing the Education of School Administrators (1992)*, and *Understanding the Principalship: Metaphorical Themes 1920s to 1990s* (with Lynn G. Beck, 1993).

1

Conceptions of Ethics in Educational Administration

We cannot expect to find in our society a single set of moral concepts. . . . Conceptual conflict is endemic in our situation because of the depth of our moral conflicts. Each of us therefore has to choose both with whom we wish to be morally bound and by what ends, rules, and virtues we wish to be guided.

Alasdair MacIntyre from *A Short History of Ethics* (1966), p. 268

In the recent rebirth of interest in educational ethics, two themes stand out in the area of school administration. The first is a belief that education is "invested from the outset with a moral character" (Hodgkinson, 1991, p. 26). The second, a natural extension of the first, is the belief that educators must become aware of the ethical implications of their work and that they must continually strive to make and be guided by morally sound decisions and to encourage others to do the same. Interestingly, despite agreements on these ideas, scholars seem to differ—at times slightly and at times rather dramatically—in their interpretations and understandings of ethics and its relationship to practice and decision making.

As we sought to understand the current status of ethics in educational administration programs, we realized that we needed some way of thinking about the various conceptions of ethics, values, and morals as they relate to educational leadership. After pondering the various recommendations for the development of "moral imagination and interpersonal competence" (Greenfield, 1987, p. 70), we discovered that

1

authors writing on this topic seem to think about ethics in one of two general ways. Many concentrate upon identifying, explicating, analyzing, and justifying certain principles or "concepts used by administrators in ethical reasoning and [in] the process of ethical reflection itself" (Strike, Haller, & Soltis, 1988, p. 6). Others, taking a slightly different approach, assume that

> reasoning and decision making are only a part of what morality encompasses. It is concerned with the way in which we typically regard ourselves and others (and the social and physical world in which we live) as well as how we act; with the range of stable dispositions, attitudes, and emotions that incline us to see and act as we do. (Crittenden, 1984, p. 18)

Those holding this view tend to stress the need for experiences within preparation programs that shape not only the thought of administrators but also their perceptions, beliefs, assumptions, emotions, and commitments. In the sections that follow, we discuss these two broad ways of thinking about ethics, noting several more specific interpretations and applications of these concepts as manifested in the work of several authors who have influenced the preparation programs we examined.[1]

This chapter opens with a general discussion of the notion that ethics provide principles to guide administrators toward morally sound decisions and continues with an examination of three ways this assumption has influenced efforts to prepare ethical leaders. We first discuss scholarship predicated upon the idea that knowledge of various philosophical principles can assist administrators in "the process of ethical reasoning" (Strike et al., 1988, p. xi). Next, we look at efforts to equip administrators to understand and interpret "relevant laws and regulations" (Crittenden, 1984, p. 28). Finally, we explore work that concentrates upon the importance of professional codes of conduct in the development of ethical practice.

In the second section, the focus shifts to an examination of the idea that ethics provide a perspective on educational purposes, roles, and practices and that the development of ethical leaders requires cultivating certain fundamental ways of thinking and understanding. As in the previous section, we begin with a general discussion of the idea that ethical persons perceive the world, their roles, and others in certain distinctive ways. We then look at three manifestations of this view in administrative literature. First, we discuss scholarship that suggests that moral leaders will seek to identify education's deepest and finest purposes and allow these purposes to influence their thinking and acting. Next, we look at the work of authors who stress the importance of understanding education as a social enterprise and who argue that ethical administrators will seek to uphold certain political values and ideas. Finally, we turn our attention to those who stress that moral leadership requires seeing schools as inhabited by persons and making decisions and engaging in actions that honor, respect, and support individuals.

Ethics as Principles, Providing Guidelines for Decision Making and Problem Solving

Much of the recent attention to ethics has arisen in response to a growing awareness of the complex dilemmas facing educational leaders. Today, administrators must discover ways to work with teachers, students, and parents representing a wide range of circumstances. Within their schools, they must cultivate a shared vision, meaningful and coherent professional and personal experiences, and a sense of membership in a community of learning with persons who may have some profound differences in living conditions, values, and beliefs. Complicating this challenge is the fact that many of the norms, ideals, and assumptions that once provided a fairly stable framework to guide leaders are under attack (e.g., Mitchell, 1990a).

In an effort to identify ways educators might respond to multifaceted challenges and value-linked conflicts, some scholars have emphasized the importance of identifying principles that can guide leaders in untangling quandaries and resolving dilemmas. For some, these take the form of "moral principles" that can be applied to specific cases to provide guidance in "ethical reasoning" (Strike et al., 1988, p. 4). Others look to policies and laws emanating from some superordinate governing body for help in solving complicated problems (see, for example, Cohen, 1976; Mitchell, 1990a; 1990b). Still others emphasize the importance of professionals' developing their own codes of conduct to guide them in the decision-making process (Kultgen, 1988).

Ethics as Philosophical Principles

In his essay, "The Moral Context of Decision Making in Education," Brian Crittenden (1984) argues for the existence of "at least some moral values that are generally recognized and that can be upheld objectively" (p. 16). For him these values center around "respect for human life" and include "such notions as love, loyalty, justice, honesty, courage, . . . generosity, . . . truth telling and promise keeping, and [respect for] political authority, property, and family" (p. 16). Because these values are linked to "common needs and capacities of human beings, to the characteristic condition on which the flourishing of life depends, and to human experience" (p. 22), Crittenden asserts that universal principles supportive of basic human values can be developed and that these can provide guidance to educational leaders seeking to make moral decisions and "to rationally justify their decisions as thoroughly as possible" (p. 35).

In his discussion, Crittenden concentrates on the possibility that principles *do* exist that can provide criteria for administrators seeking to determine "the appropriate educational means for achieving a predetermined end" (p. 33). He does not offer a comprehensive discussion of specific principles, however. Strike et al. (1988), following Crittenden's line of thinking, do offer such a discussion. In *The Ethics of School Administration*, these authors draw a distinction between "*facts, moral principles,* and *preferences*" (p. 36, emphasis in the original) and demonstrate the interplay of these three phenomena in the decision-making process. Presenting cases containing an array of facts about a problematic condition, Strike and his coauthors invite readers to consider their own preferences and those of others in the situation, and they define and discuss concepts related to the cases in question and suggest ways that certain ethical principles can guide leaders in evaluating preferences, interpreting concepts, and making decisions. Two of the central ethical principles discussed are the principle of benefit maximization and the principle of equal respect. The first of these "holds that, whenever we are faced with a choice, the best and most just decision is the one that results in the most good or the greatest benefit for the most people" (p. 16). The latter, in turn, "requires that we act in ways that respect the equal worth of moral agents. It requires that we regard human beings as having intrinsic worth and treat them accordingly" (p. 17). Using these and other moral guidelines—such as the principle of equal treatment and the principle of noninterference—Strike et al. (1988)

demonstrate the ways moral principles might inform and guide educational leaders who must make "hard choices . . . under complex and ambiguous circumstances" (p. 3). Throughout their book, they are not pretending to claim that there is "one right answer to every moral dilemma" (p. 3). Rather, they are attempting to assist administrators in making good decisions and wise choices that are based upon broadly accepted moral principles and not merely upon the personal preferences of the decision maker.

Similarly, building upon the work of Gastil (1977), Sergiovanni (1980) offers a set of "pluralistic criteria" to guide decision makers in "problem analysis and [in] selection from among alternatives" (p. 3) in the quest for "solutions for concrete, practical problems" (Hills, 1978, p. 2; quoted in Sergiovanni, 1980, p. 16).[2] He suggests that four principles form a sound and helpful framework within which leaders can consider various options. The first, concerning the value of utility, asserts that administrators must be "concerned with the practical, with social maximization, with costs and benefits, and with other standards of production and achievement" (p. 4). Sergiovanni's second principle emphasizes the notion of "transcendence" (p. 4). In his discussion of this concept, he writes that decision makers must assess "the capacity of an alternative to increase the potential of society for achieving humanness in the pursuit of happiness" (p. 4) and calls on educational leaders to "give attention to the potential of each [possible decision] to help individuals, organizations, the community, and society to move beyond the ordinary, to grow to new levels of understanding, to higher standards of operation" (p. 4). Sergiovanni next concentrates upon justice: "As educational administrators and policy makers evaluate decision alternatives, they [should] give attention to the extent each provides for a just distribution of benefits" (p. 4). Finally, he asserts that, "As decision makers and policy makers evaluate decision alternatives on the basis of utility, transcendence, and justice, they should consider as well the ethical questions which surface" (p. 5). Acknowledging that these questions are often difficult to answer, he nevertheless argues that morally sound consideration of solutions to dilemmas must take into account the boundaries or limits imposed by personal and professional ethical commitments and beliefs. Like Strike et al. (1988), Sergiovanni does not present these principles as a formula. Rather, he suggests that they can serve as useful guidelines for educators confronting complex problems which compel decisions and solutions.

Ethics as Embodied in Laws and Public Policies

Crittenden (1984) suggests that persons seeking to understand the ethical challenges facing school leaders would do well to "to distinguish between the basic social morality—the values and practices without which society could hardly survive and would certainly not be tolerable—and the comprehensible bodies of moral belief about what is good or desirable for social and individual human life" (p. 18). In his view, the task of an educational leader is that of a trustee of a public, social good, and persons who undertake this task must allow themselves to be guided by certain tenets of public morality:

> As a minimum, the basic social morality includes the practices of justice, truth telling and honesty, concern for others at least to the extent of avoiding the infliction of injury, mutual help in satisfying essential physical and cultural needs, and the willingness to recognize the claims that others make on us on the basis of these practices. (pp. 18-19)

Crittenden asserts that, within pluralistic societies,

> it is obvious that decisions in the domain of public morality should be based on the principles of the essential core of social morality together with those values on which the policy of moral pluralism itself directly depends (personal freedom, the equal worth of all individuals as moral agents, tolerance of diverse ways of thinking and acting, the use of non-violent persuasions). In the political and legal systems of the society *these values are translated into more specific principles and procedures (for example, consent of the governed, majority rule, due process of law, [and] various specific rights of freedom.* (p. 21, emphasis added)

In his view, public administrators are thus under obligation to seek guidance from principles and procedures embodied in laws and public policies as they make decisions. Indeed, he asserts:

> In many of the decisions, general as well as particular, made by educational administrators, the application or interpretation of

legally binding directives is the main issue. . . . In moral terms, educational administrators have a duty to ensure that the decisions they make accord with the relevant laws and regulations. The scope of their authority even at the highest levels, is itself at least broadly determined by law. (p. 28)

Crittenden suggests that, in a society that has accepted certain fundamental values (i.e., respect for individuals), laws established by representatives of its citizens can and should serve as moral directives. To be sure, he does not claim that educational leaders must blindly and unthinkingly enforce laws as "clear-cut rules" (p. 31). Rather, he sees the task of administrators as one of interpreting laws and public policies in ways that meet the needs of particular situations and remain true to the principles undergirding the legal directives.

Beauchamp and Childress (1984), although they do not use the words "laws" and "public policies," frame their discussion of moral decision making in ways that support Crittenden's assertions. In essence, they argue for "the place of rules" (p. 57) in administrative thinking and reject the notion that situational ethics can provide adequate guidance for persons facing difficult and complex dilemmas. Their advocacy of "some rules and derivative principles" is based upon belief in the existence of some "virtually exceptionless or absolute principles" (p. 59). These authors suggest that some of these absolutes—those that "refer to traits of character whose development and expression are always good"—are likely to be covered by philosophical principles. However, they also suggest that many of the absolutes find their expression in public laws with clearly defined terminology (i.e., murder as unjustified killing) that have "exceptions built into them" (p. 59). Further, Beauchamp and Childress assert that rights—"justified claims that individual and groups can make upon others or upon society" (p. 61)—and duties and obligations established by these rights are, within democratic societies such as ours, defined in laws and policies and guarded by constitutionally established processes for interpreting and changing legal directives. Thus, like Crittenden, Beauchamp and Childress argue that educational administrators in societies whose governments are committed to certain fundamental principles, such as justice, tolerance, and respect for and fair treatment of all persons, can and should look to laws and public policies for ethical guidance.

Codes of Ethics as Guides to Decisions

The beliefs that ethics are embodied in legal directives and that ethical leaders have a mandate to look to policies for assistance as they seek pathways through troublesome situations presuppose several things. First, they assume that people—functioning collectively through some form of democratic government—are equipped to determine the ways individuals should act and interact. Second, they assume that laws and policies as crafted by representatives of individuals will embody the intentions of society and, further, that they will create mechanisms for protest and change if those are desirable. Finally, they presume that educational leaders are responsible to enact and support the will of society as expressed in laws and public policies. A related view of ethics shifts the onus for establishing ethical rules and guidelines from society to the educational profession. Those holding this view emphasize the importance of professional codes of ethics in decision making.

In *Ethics and Professionalism* (1988), John Kultgen examines, in some detail, the belief that professions, because they "represent the highest level of competence in our civilization," and because they are dedicated to "truth and service [in ways that] cut across political and cultural boundaries" (p. x), are the institutions best able to provide ethical guidance to their members. Surveying the history of this belief, he discusses the influence of Durkheim (1950/1957) and Whitehead (1933), "the two men who inaugurated modern thinking about professions" (Kultgen, 1988, p. 43). Kultgen suggests that these scholars held "utopian conceptions of professionalism" (p. 43), in that they assumed both that membership in a profession means that one possesses a degree of "competence to attain those ends whose immediate dominance is evident to enlightened wisdom" (Whitehead, 1933, pp. 71-79) and that such membership accords "moral authority" (Whitehead, 1933, pp. 71-79) to such a person. A logical extension of this idea is that the collective insights of individual authorities carry moral weight and can provide guidelines for the "happy coordination of individual emotions, purposes, affections, and actions" (Whitehead, 1933, pp. 71-79) in the pursuit of "freedom, truth, and beauty" (Kultgen, 1988, p. 46). Thus Durkheim and Whitehead helped to establish a belief that professions can serve in at least a limited way as moral *milieux*. With the right ideals they can improve the way people do their work, encourage them to consider the social consequences, and cultivate a heightened and more enlightened commitment to the common good. (Kultgen, 1988, p. 45)

Recent decades have witnessed much cynicism regarding the beliefs that "human beings are so constituted that under favorable conditions they will take the moral point of view" (Kultgen, 1988, pp. 47-48) and that professions provide such conditions. However, Kultgen argues that these ideas do contain a "valid kernel" (p. 45) that must not be overlooked. He then examines various ways that professions and their codes of ethics can provide "guidance for those practitioners who have not thought through moral issues . . . [and who face] difficult dilemmas" (p. 216). Indeed, he asserts that "debates over confidentiality, conflict of interest, bribery, paternalism, whistle-blowing, credit for the work of others, social responsibilities, etc." (p. 216) require "hard thinking and searching dialogue" (p. 216) and that a code can summarize the results of such activities for persons who do not have the time and inclination to engage in them:

A rational code would contain the results individuals would have reached for themselves if they had reasoned objectively long enough on an adequate base of experience. If such a code is available, it relieves professionals of most of the burden of ethical inquiry. After all, their primary responsibility is to heal, counsel, minister, design, etc. not to puzzle over ethical questions. Most in matter of fact do not reflect on ethics until faced with difficult questions, when the pressure of action prevents careful thought. It would simplify their moral universe to have solutions at hand which had been worked on the collective experience and wisdom of the moral community. (p. 216)

To be sure, Kultgen does not suggest that codes can be treated as formulas or prescriptions and he emphasizes "the need for personal judgment" (p. 216) on the part of those looking to them. He does, however, propose that codes can provide important and useful guidelines regarding ideals, behaviors, and decisions.

Ethics as Perspectives Informing
Perceptions, Character, and Beliefs

Certain assumptions undergird and unite the views of ethics discussed in the preceding sections. For example, each presupposes that the primary function of ethics is to guide individuals as they approach dilemmas that require hard choices between competing values (Pincoffs, 1971). Each view also tends to emphasize the importance of a systematic and rational approach to ethical behavior, for each presents a set of tenets that can guide the thinking of decision makers. The preceding views also presume that a function of ethics is to help individuals avoid being swayed by their emotions and personal interests, concerns, and beliefs as they seek to choose morally sound strategies and activities from a range of alternatives (Hauerwas & Burrell, 1977).

The belief that ethics are and should be concerned with "action-guiding rules and principles, choice and decision, universality and impartiality, and obligation and right action" (Blum, 1991, p. 701) has been explicitly or implicitly accepted by many who write about the ethics of educational leaders. However, a small but growing number of individuals have begun to examine the moral challenges facing administrators in ways that suggest an expanded notion of ethics. In the sections that follow, we discuss three themes that permeate the scholarship that assumes that ethics inform not only decision making but the perceptions, character, and beliefs of educators operating individually and corporately. The first theme emphasizes that moral leadership requires a consideration of the fundamental purposes of education, of the nature of schools as institutions, and of the roles and responsibilities of educational leaders. Those advocating this perspective (e.g., Greenfield, 1988; Hodgkinson, 1991; Sergiovanni, 1992; Starratt, 1991) see ethics as informing administrators' understandings of themselves as moral agents and of their schools as moral agencies. The second theme concentrates more specifically upon the responsibility of schools to contribute to the public good. A number of scholars (e.g., Giroux, 1988; Purpel, 1989) stress that ethics must assist educators in gaining a robust understanding of the common or public good and in determining morally sound ways to pursue this good. The third theme is anchored in the belief that persons, not principles, provide the fundamental *raison d'etre* of applied moral philosophy. Those articulating this idea (e.g., Beck, 1992, 1994a; Gilligan, 1982; Noddings, 1984, 1992) insist that ethics should encourage and assist persons in developing lasting commitments to understand and care for others.

Ethics as a Way of Understanding Purposes, Roles and Institutions

Drawing upon the work of Iris Murdoch (1970), Lawrence Blum (1991) asserts that traditional notions of ethics, which "focus on action-guiding rules and principles, on choice and decision, on universality and impartiality, and on obligation and right action" (p. 701), fail to take into account the facts that "in any given situation moral perception comes on the scene prior to moral judgment; moral perception can lead to moral action outside the operation of judgment entirely; and, more generally, perception involves moral capacities not encompassed by moral judgments" (p. 702). For Blum, developing these capacities requires cultivating the ability to recognize in situations those details that are morally significant. However, it also requires understanding the panoply of purpose (including moral purpose) undergirding human interactions. Thus Blum argues that ethics must be concerned with how people perceive themselves, others, and their shared experiences. Hauerwas and Burrell (1977) arrive at a similar conclusion when they assert that contemporary ethicists' concentration "on problems—situations in which it is hard to know what to do—as paradigmatic concerns for moral analysis" (p. 18) is inadequate. Such emphasis fails to realize the ethical significance of the capacity to identify certain situations as problematic, to assume that one has a right and responsibility to seek some kind of solution, to perceive a repertoire of alternatives from which to choose, to make right choices informed by one's "virtue and character" (p. 20). Like Blum, they suggest that ethics must be concerned with developing right ways of thinking about people and their relationships.

In recent years several scholars have written about the ethics of educational leadership in ways that are consonant with the conceptions of Blum (1991) and Hauerwas and Burrell (1977). Two scholars whose discussions of ethics demonstrate expanded ways of thinking are T. B. Greenfield (1979) and Christopher Hodgkinson (1991). Greenfield's insistence that organizations are born out of the beliefs, emotions, thoughts, volitions, and experiences of individuals emphasizes certain ways of understanding leadership. In his view, the tasks of all members of organizations—especially of leaders—have moral dimensions, because they require, at every point, working with, protecting, and honoring people. Greenfield (1979) writes that leaders who function in ethically sound or right ways must "engage in a continuing process of discovery aimed at gaining an understanding of ourselves and of others" (p. 109). Thus, both in his approach to organizational study and in his claim that scholars and leaders must pursue *understanding* as a foundation to ethical behavior, Greenfield exemplifies the idea that ethics are rightly concerned with the ways individuals think about themselves, others, and the organizations and experiences they share.

In *Educational Leadership: The Moral Art* (1991), Hodgkinson, like Greenfield, suggests that administrators must be aware that because education has "relevance to all aspects of the human condition, [it] is also invested from the outset with a moral character" (p. 27). He argues that leaders must be guided by more than "mere pragmatism, positivism, philistinism, and careerism" (p. 165)—that they must develop "extraordinary value sensitivity" (p. 164). For Hodgkinson, this requires continuous reflection upon the values undergirding educational efforts and upon the role of leaders in honoring those values. In order to encourage this, he presents new ways of thinking about the fundamental purposes of schooling.

In recent works (1992, 1993a, 1993b), Sergiovanni, too, argues that the ethical practice of leadership requires wrestling with foundational questions. In *Moral Leadership: Getting to the Heart of School Improvement* (1992), he challenges scholars and practitioners to think about the meanings they attach to words such as "education," "schools," and "leadership." In his view, ethical practice, i.e., "doing the right things" (p. 4), requires educators to commit themselves to developing a "virtuous school," that is both "moral and effective" (p. 107). As they cultivate such a school, Sergiovanni challenges leaders to concentrate not merely upon what they do and think, but also upon who they *are* and upon what they believe and feel. He further asks both scholars and practitioners to think seriously about "the basic theories and root metaphors that shape the way we understand schools and shape the way we understand leadership and management within them" (1993b, p. 2). Sergiovanni suggests that, historically, education has borrowed "its fundamental frames for thinking about how schools should be structured and coordinated, how compliance within them should be achieved, what leadership is, and how it works" (p. 2) and that educators have thus passively allowed others to define their work (see also Miklos, 1990). He sees in this passivity a moral failure that can be rectified as scholars and practitioners begin "to decide which theory should domi-nate which spheres of our lives" (p. 20). In making these claims, he insists that ethics must do more than assist administrators in making decisions and that, as a field, ethics must help scholars and practitioners understand the purposes, values, and commitments behind their work.

Yet another scholar who concurs with this expanded notion of ethics is Robert J. Starratt (1991). In "Building an Ethical School: A Theory for Practice in Educational Leadership," he argues that the primary ethical task facing school leaders "is to establish an ethical school environment in which education can take place ethically" (p. 187). Starratt suggests that administrators seeking to fulfill this task allow themselves to be guided by a "multi-dimensional ethic" (p. 199) that emphasizes, simultaneously, caring, critique, and justice. In his view, these three ethical perspectives are needed by leaders seeking to react morally to specific dilemmas and challenges as well as to engage proactively in the comprehensive task of the "building of an ethical school as an integral part of a national effort to restructure schools" (p. 199). For Starratt, a commitment to multiple ethical perspectives will promote the development of "an ethical consciousness" (p. 201). Such a consciousness will enable leaders to avoid being "captured by senti-mentality, by rationalistic simplification, or by social naivete" (p. 200) and to approach each and every activity in ways that honor individuals and their varied communities.

Ethics as Politics

A number of scholars, although not disagreeing with the perspec-tives of Sergiovanni, Starratt, and others cited in the previous section, emphasize the importance of educators' adopting a more specific ethical perspective. Henry Giroux (1988) and David Purpel (1989) are among those most vocal in calling on administrators, teachers, and those who work with them in colleges and universities to recognize that schools must play a key role in the development of a just and caring society. For these scholars, ethics, politics, and schooling go hand in hand, because all, ideally, should provide mechanisms for improving the human condition. In his call for a "politics of ethics" (p. 37), Giroux asks educators to consider the ways their pedagogies, curricula, and organizational structures further social and political ends. Addition-ally, he challenges them to allow a "radical theory of ethics" (p. 59) to guide them as they develop "norms of solidarity, sympathy, caring, friendship, and love" and as they "promote the material conditions and forms of solidarity that point to a better life . . . [and] contribute to actualizing what Agnes Heller (1985) has called the universal values of life and freedom" (p. 59).

David Purpel's (1989) perspective on ethics is similar to Giroux's in that he sees "intimate relationships among society, culture, and education" (p. x). He contends that most people operating within these three spheres have, in the past, ignored the moral and spiritual implications of their activities. This, in his view, has led to "an impoverished civic discourse that celebrates freedom as a form of possessive individualism and treats the concept of democracy as if it were at odds with the notion of community" (p. xv). Purpel asserts that ethics of social justice and compassion must be conjoined as educators reshape both the structures and the cultures of schools so they can become "just, loving, and joyous communit[ies]" (p. 123) in which all persons can grow and learn. He further asserts that, as educators and others give voice to "our mythic goals, our sacred aspirations, and our moral commitments" (p. 122) within schools, we will help to move the larger world toward the realization of "a society based on a serious and continuing commitment to peace, joy, love, social justice, equality, and community" (p. 152).

Ethics Grounded in a Commitment to Persons

Carol Gilligan's watershed book, *In a Different Voice* (1982), expressed a notion of ethics that, in the past decade, has received a fair amount of attention in educational circles. Gilligan's research challenged the Kohlbergian concept that the highest level of moral development is reached when a person looks to universal ethical principles for guidance in solving moral dilemmas. Troubled by the fact that Kohlberg's research had been exclusively with males, Gilligan replicated the studies that led to the formulation of his theories, but this time with young women. She found that many of her subjects were aware of impersonal principles but rejected them as the pivotal guides in solving ethical dilemmas, preferring instead to ground their responses in a commitment to solve problems in ways that were most beneficial to individual persons. Gilligan posits an alternative way of thinking about ethics, suggesting that a commitment to care for persons and to promote their growth and development to the greatest extent possible can provide a viable ethical perspective which is as mature as an objective, principle-driven orientation.

Nel Noddings (1984, 1988a, 1988b, 1992) has been a key figure in developing a model of the ways in which an ethical perspective centered on caring and on the promotion of personal development might influence education. She suggests that such an orientation would shape conceptions of educational purposes and pedagogical and organizational strategies for achieving those purposes. For Noddings, schools must focus, first and foremost, on promoting the development, health, and happiness of individual human beings and, because persons are fundamentally relational, they must also focus on developing capacities for "interpersonal caring" (1992, p. 18).

Noddings suggests that this focus, influenced throughout by an ethic of care, would in all likelihood lead to many changes in our schools. For example, she argues that teaching and learning, influenced by caring, would be much more individualized than they are currently. Asserting that "caring teachers listen and respond differentially to their students" (p. 19), she writes:

> We need to give up the notion of an ideal of the educated person and replace it with a multiplicity of models designed to accommodate the multiple capacities and interests of students. We need to recognize multiple identities. For example, an 11th grader may be a black, a woman, a teenager, a Smith, an American, a New Yorker, a Methodist, a person who loves math, and so on. As she exercises these identities, she may use different languages, adopt different postures, relate differently to those around her. But whoever she is at a given moment, what she is engaged in, she needs—as we all do—to be cared for. Her need for care may require formal respect, informal interaction, expert advice, just a flicker of recognition, or sustained affection. (Noddings, 1992, p. 173)

In addition to introducing more personal pedagogies, Noddings notes that an ethic of care would influence thinking about curricular issues: "I have argued that education should be organized around themes of care rather than the traditional disciplines. All students should be engaged in a general education that guides them in caring for self, intimate others, global others, plants, animals, and the environment, the human-made world and ideas" (1992, p. 173). She also asserts that such an ethic would shape our understandings of assessment: "We should move away from the question, Has Johnny learned X? to the far more pertinent question, What has Johnny learned?" (1992, p. 179). Noddings suggests that teachers, principals, and parents should join with students to evaluate the answer to this question and then "roll up [their] sleeves and work together to accomplish what [they] deem important" (p. 180).

Drawing upon many of the ideas offered by Noddings, Beck (1992, 1994a) concentrates upon the ways an ethic of care, with its focus upon people and their development, can and should inform the practice and preparation of educational administrators. She asserts that this ethic's concepts of the nature and purpose of humans and their communities are philosophically and practically appropriate for schools and for their leaders. After defining this ethic in some detail, Beck explores its relevance for principals, superintendents, and other school executives. For example, she presents research that suggests relationships among a caring ethos, student achievement, and teachers' sense of efficacy, and she offers evidence that the orientation, commitments, and behaviors of administrators can do much to cultivate or destroy a nurturing, supportive culture. She then discusses roles that a caring administrator might embrace and suggests that such a person would seek to be "a values-driven organizer," "a creative and capable pedagogue," and "cultivator of a nurturing culture" (1994a, p. 78). In Beck's view, schools exist for people—to promote their growth and health and that of their various social networks. Thus she contends that ethical perspectives that focus upon personal and community well-being are consistent with the fundamental purposes of education and appropriate to guide educational leaders.

Concluding Thoughts

As MacIntyre (1966) notes in the quotation that opens this chapter, we do not possess "a single set of moral concepts" (p. 268) to use in discussions of ethics. We assert that this plurality extends beyond multiple understandings of concepts and encompasses the varied ways we think about ethics and their relationships to personal and professional interactions. We contend that a robust understanding of the ways educational administration programs are addressing issues of ethics requires that we examine not only course content and pedagogical strategies, but also the assumptions about ethics that guide programmatic decisions. In subsequent chapters, we will seek to ground the analysis of our research findings in the framework presented in this chapter.

Notes

1. In dividing an understanding of ethics into categories, we do not mean to imply that these are neatly circumscribed, philosophical camps. They are not, and most authors we cite make no claim to have discovered the "real" or "true" meaning of ethics. They do, however, emphasize different ways of thinking. These emphases provided the basis for our division of this section into two major categories with three subfoci in each.

2. In later work (e.g., 1992, 1993a, 1993b), Sergiovanni, although not denying the importance of rational decision making, tends to emphasize the ways ethical commitments provide perspectives on education's deepest purposes and underlying metaphors and to argue that these commitments must shape the being as well as the thinking of school leaders.

2

The Place of Ethics:
A Historical Perspective

*There is a problem, namely, that inadequate attention has been
given to the moral and ethical components and dimensions of
administrative action.*

Erwin Miklos from *Ethical Aspects of Administrative
Action (1977-1978), p. 4*

In Chapter 1, we provided a broad overview of ethics—establishing
the context for our analysis of the place of ethics in educational programs for school leaders. In this chapter, we provide a historical
perspective on this issue, revealing how ethics has (or has not) been
woven into the fabric of administrator training over the last 125 years.
Although the spotlight is on preparation programs, we will, out of
necessity, ground this discussion within the larger context of the
profession that, as Newlon (1934), Callahan (1962), and Watson (1977)
have shown, is itself nested in the prevailing culture of American
society. We begin with a brief description of the place of ethics—
broadly conceived—in the life of school leaders during the 19th century. We then review the forces that throughout much of the 20th
century have redirected the focus in preparation programs away from
issues of ethics. The third section explores empirical evidence on the
extent of ethics content in training programs from 1900 to 1990. We
conclude with a discussion of what appears to be a renewed interest in
values, morals, and ethics in educational programs for school leaders.

The Era of Ideology in Preparation Programs (pre-1900)

Educators [administrators] were ministers before they were behavioral scientists. (March, 1978, p. 244)

Leadership in public education was often seen as a *calling* similar to that of church missionary. (Tyack & Hansot, 1982, p. 16, emphasis in original)

Chronicles of the development of educational administration reveal that the formal training of school administrators is a rather recent development (Campbell, Fleming, Newell, and Bennion, 1987; Gregg, 1969; Murphy, in press b; Silver, 1982). As Gregg (1960) reminds us, "little had been written before 1900 on educational administration, and formal preparation programs for school administrators had not yet been developed" (p. 20). What we do know about educational leadership in its formative stage is that it had a distinctive value focus. Kerchner (1988) refers to this time as the "evangelical period" in school administration. Tyack and Hansot (1982) talk about an "aristocracy of character." And Callahan and Button (1964) employ the term "philosopher-educator" to describe the 19th century school leader. The doctrine of educational administration as applied philosophy that held sway from 1885 to 1905

> asserted that truth, concerning all things and all matters, was eternal and to be discovered. As in all other fields, this was necessary in education. It therefore followed that the learned administrator, who could discover relevant truths, was the best authority on all matters concerning education, and that the problem of administration was the application of philosophical knowledge to schools. (Button, 1966, p. 218)

This doctrine, "with its emphasis on eternal wisdom and moral judgment, made the administrator into something like the clergyman and borrowed from him some of the clergyman's status" (Button, 1966, p. 219).

Forces Pushing Ethics Offstage[1]

By the early 1960s, the second major root of the field (values and ethics), like education before it, had atrophied. (Murphy, 1992a, p. 96)

In the early 1900s, forces were set in motion that were to have a significant impact upon conceptions of educational leadership and upon the focus of preparation programs designed to educate school administrators. The United States was moving rapidly from an agricultural to an industrial society, a change that would signal the death knell for the prevailing view of superintendents and principals as philosopher-educators. "The great material achievements of industrial capitalism in the late nineteenth century" led to a growing infatuation with issues of commerce, "the rise of the business and industrial group to a position of prestige and influence [and] the saturation of America with business-industrial values and practices" (Callahan & Button, 1964, p. 77).

As usual, educational administration responded quickly to this changing social context (Beck & Murphy, 1993; Callahan, 1962; Campbell et al., 1987). Unbridled enthusiasm for business and industry, and particularly for the principles of scientific management promulgated by Frederick Taylor and his followers, resulted in the emergence of a new conception of school leaders. Gone was the view of the leader as a moral agent. In its stead stood a picture of the school superintendent as a businessperson, as a captain of commerce (Button, 1966; Callahan, 1962; Cooper & Boyd, 1987), a view that led to a number of important outcomes. First, "it allied the administrator with a high status group, the businessmen" (Button, 1966, p. 220). Second, it enhanced the status of administrators by cloaking their work in an aura of "scientific respectability" (Callahan & Button, 1964, p. 83). Third, and most important for our purposes here, it replaced the moral and educational compass by which school leaders navigated with a ledger book: "The new doctrine of school administration as management defined school administration as being like the management of a business or factory. . . . The appropriate basis for decision-making then was ideally a fiscal one" (Button, 1966, p. 219).

Forty years later, two variables—politics and science—that were to result in the profession becoming even further divorced from values and ethics were added to the decision-making algorithm. As the pre-scriptive era (1900-1945) in educational administration drew to a close, schooling was widely held to be beyond the fray of politics. Beginning with the onset of the behavioral science era (1946-1985), however, the view of the school leader as a politician began to augment—and supplant—earlier views of administrators as educators and managers. The politics that dominated the field for nearly 40 years had consider-ably more to do with the authoritative allocation of power and re-sources than with the moral beacons by which such activities need to be guided.

At the same time, roughly during the years immediately following the Second World War, the fabric of American society began to change again. It embarked on a period of unchecked enthusiasm for the world of science and all things scientific—including a rather uncritical accep-tance of its ideological and epistemological underpinnings. Scientists, not businesspeople, now held center stage (Halpin, 1960). Not surpris-ingly, given the vulnerability of school leaders to larger societal forces (Callahan, 1962), the school administration profession quickly began to reconstruct itself with material from this new movement. A science of school administration began to take form. This new perspective on administration "advocated that science, cast in an objective, positivistic mould, could save the field from the philosophers, moralists, and other subjectivists" (Greenfield, 1988, p. 142):

> The new science of administration was to make a sharp distinc-tion between philosophy and science; prescribing to adminis-trators the actions they should take was seen as something distinctly different from describing and explaining adminis-tration through scientific concepts and theories. Those who adhered strictly to the new school of thought focused upon the description and explanation of administrative phenomena and avoided prescriptive statements. Thus, the authors of a major textbook on public administration published in 1950 argued that "a science (of administration) in the sense of an objective understanding of the phenomena without confusion between facts and values" is possible. The authors, therefore, concen-trated on the scientific aspects of administration and con-sciously avoided stating what government *should* do. (Culbertson, 1964, pp. 307-308)

The results of these new foci in educational administration were predictable. Despite some thoughtful, and sometimes impassioned, pleas for additional attention to ethics in educational administration (Culbertson, 1964, 1965; Farquhar, 1968; Harlow, 1962), value issues remained largely overlooked in the profession in general and were regularly ignored in preparation programs in particular.

Empirical Evidence on the State of Ethics in Preparation Programs[2]

The place of ethics in administrative theory has been relatively minor until recently. (Evers, 1992, p. 29),

Courses in ethics are rare in educational administration programmes. [This, in turn] pales in comparison with the virtual non-existence of related resources. (Kirby, Paradise, & Protti, 1992, p. 25)

Some serious homework is required if the development of ethical competence is to be fruitfully pursued in preparation programs in educational administration. (Farquhar, 1981, p. 202)

Insights into the extent of ethics instruction in preparation programs are both direct and indirect, although more often of the latter type. They are best understood within the context of the forces noted above, that is, nested in a deeper understanding of the place of values and ethics in the profession of school administration generally. Four sources are particularly relevant in addressing the issue at hand: Newlon's (1934) analysis of the state of the profession; Silver and Spuck's (1978) study of preparation programs; Farquhar's (1981) direct investigation into the place of ethics in training programs; and Norton and Levan's (1987) review of the curriculum in school leadership preparation programs.[3]

Newlon's 1934 Analysis

One of the earliest and most important pieces of evidence about the ascendancy of the technical aspects of administration and the concomitant decline in emphasis on "the fundamental social . . . problems of school administration" (p. 262) was provided by Jesse Newlon (1934) in his classic work, *Educational Administration as Social Policy*. Operating under the assumption that "one of the best criteria for judging the emphasis in the professional education of school administrators is . . . the problems in the field that have been chosen for research" (p. 260), Newlon undertook a content analysis of dissertations completed between 1910 and 1933. He concludes that departments of school administration were "principally" concerned with the "technical phases" of "the professional education of school executives" (p. 261). He reports an absence of attention to social issues and "to the social methods and techniques which their solution requires" (p. 262). Another analysis in Newlon's volume reviews the topics that professors and superintendents judged to be most important in the preparation of superintendents. This examination reveals a similar bias toward "the spheres of finance, business management, physical equipment, and the more mechanical aspects of administration, organization, personnel management, and the like" (p. 259). A third

> analysis of the contents of eighteen such textbooks published during the last fifty years . . . [reveals] that over four-fifths of the eight thousand pages are devoted to the purely executive, organizational, and legal aspects of administration. Almost the entire emphasis is on the "how" of administration. There is virtually no discussion of the "why," little critical examination of educational and social implications of the structures and procedures discussed. (p. 93)

Finally, Newlon's investigation of actual courses in school administration "shows clearly the emphasis on the technical and the factual, the external. Most of the topics have to do with the mechanics of administration" (p. 99).

Silver and Spuck's 1978 Study

In the 1975-1976 academic year, under the auspices of the University Council for Educational Administration (UCEA), Paula Silver and Dennis Spuck—with a series of colleagues—undertook the most comprehensive survey of preparation programs in the United States in the history of the profession. Their study, which employed a variety of investigators and was nested in a larger international research design,[4] shed a good deal of light on the place of ethics in school administration. For our purposes here, the key part of the questionnaire that was distributed to professors and students asked respondents "to indicate which areas were emphasized in the greatest number of student programs" (Alkire, 1978, p. 55). What makes this assessment particularly potent is that it is especially sensitive to the presence of ethics in training programs. That is, it does not examine whether programs have developed separate courses in ethics (a weak test for the presence of ethics), but only whether the topic of ethics is an area of emphasis in student programs (a strong test for the presence of ethics).[5] It is particularly enlightening then to note that from a rather comprehensive list of 40 topic areas from which respondents could select, none dealt with ethics—or with related areas such as values, moral issues in education, etc. Thus the design of the study itself reveals a noticeable lack of emphasis on ethics in school administration preparation programs—one that was confirmed by the 258 department chairs, 633 additional professors of educational administration, and 904 students who responded to the survey (Silver & Spuck, 1978).

Farquhar's 1981 Investigation

Long an advocate for the place of the humanities in educational administration, in 1978 Robin Farquhar undertook a study "to determine whether or not major university Departments of Educational Administration are offering learning opportunities concerned with ethics and, if so, why, what, for whom, how, by whom, and with what results?" (1981, p. 195). Three things are noteworthy about this analysis. First, it is the only study conducted to date that directly examines the role of ethics in preparation programs. Second, by assessing learning opportunities rather than courses, Farquhar provided the field with a particularly sensitive (strong) measure of the robustness of ethics instruction. Third, he believed that his sample—the 48 UCEA member schools at the time—would "provide a reasonable reflection of the 'leading edge' in this field" (1981, p. 195). In short, if the results in these institutions were not encouraging, conditions elsewhere were likely to be even worse.

Farquhar's basic conclusion is that attention to ethics in educational administration preparation programs is conspicuous by its absence:

> Eighteen replies were received from the 48 universities contacted, a response rate of 37.5%. One suspects that the vast majority of those who did not reply had nothing to say on the subject. Of those that did reply, the comments of seven may be summarized as follows: ethics is an important topic and a neglected one; we don't do much, or anything, specifically in this area at our institution. (1981, p. 195)

Those who did claim to highlight ethics in their preparation programs fell into two groups: "those [7 schools] reporting that the subject of ethics is integrated throughout much of their programs, and those [4 schools] reporting distinct program components designed deliberately to focus on ethics" (1981, p. 196). The integration group respondents broke out into two subgroups: two schools that "endeavor consciously to integrate ethics into much of what they teach" (1981, p. 196) and five schools in which "to the extent that ethics are treated it is done in an effortless and incidental way" (1981, p. 196).[6]

Norton and Levan's 1987 Review

Scott Norton and Frederick Levan's (1987) work at the UCEA Program Center for Preparation Programs on "doctoral studies of students in educational administration programs in UCEA member institutions" (p. 21), although not targeting directly the topic of ethics, provides a useful (but weak)[7] measure of the state of instruction in this area at the time of transition from the scientific to the dialectic era in school administration (Murphy, 1992a).[8] By analyzing programs of study from 78 students, Norton and Levan developed seven groups of coursework, three of which are relevant to our analysis here: courses in educational administration, foundations/general education courses and cognate coursework. Of the 665 educational administration courses completed by these 78 students, not a single one has a title that would suggest a focus on ethics or values. There also appears to be little evidence of attention to ethics in the general education area: "[O]nly five Foundations courses were common to as many as five students' programs in the Ed.D. degree" (Norton & Levan, 1987, p. 22). Only one of these, Philosophy of Education, would appear to be a home for serious discussion of ethical issues. Likewise, there is little indication in the data from the Norton and Levan study that cognate area coursework is focused on ethics.

Thus the overall picture is one in which it is difficult—if not impossible—to see evidence of meaningful attention to issues of ethics in preparation programs in school administration. For much of the past century, the focus of preparation programs has taken prospective school administrators further and further away from what many would consider to be a critical foundation for effective educational leadership. At the same time, as we exit the behavioral science era, there is increasing evidence of renewed interest in ethics, values, and morals in educational administration in general and in preparation programs in particular. In the last section of this chapter, we turn our attention to this changing landscape of the profession. We review some of the forces that appear to be shaping a renewed concern for ethics, and we examine evidence that supports or contradicts claims for this rebirth of interest.

Renewed Interest

> The fourth trend toward which educational administration as a field of inquiry appears to be moving [is to] a greater concern with values and especially with equity. (Willower, 1988, pp. 729-730)

> My main point about these three recent developments in educational administration is not only that they are related but that they also seem to have a common source. They all appear rooted in the necessity of and desire for a renewed discourse on values in educational administration. (Slater, 1991, p. 18)

Rekindling Interest: The Context for Change

As we noted in Chapter 1, renewed attention to ethics in educational leadership is nested within a heightened concern for values in society in general and in education in particular. As the United States moves from an industrial to a post-industrial society, the deleterious consequences of this era—"a moral breakdown in society" (Shapiro & Smith-Rosenberg, 1989, p. 200)—to individuals and to groups are receiving considerable scrutiny. In particular, inequities of wealth, power, and status are being attacked with increased frequency. Critiques are most pointed when these issues are examined within the contexts of race, ethnicity, and gender. The widespread legitimization of the women's movement and a heightened focus on the civil rights agenda are tangible outcomes of these concerns.

Education, in turn, has begun to focus on the moral dimensions of schooling. In a direct sense, this ethics agenda is an extension of the critiques noted above—a condemnation of the way the inequities of wealth, power, and status play out in schools. The recent assault on the unequal distribution of the valued outcomes of schooling, first voiced by advocates in the effective schools movement (Murphy, 1992b), as well as concurrent attacks on the unequal allocation of the input and process variables in schooling that help explain student learning (Murphy & Hallinger, 1989) are the most central lines of work in this area. Methods of assigning students to schools and procedures for allocating funds (see Kozol, 1991) are the salient issues for those scholars who focus on input variables. Strategies used to group students for learning is the topic of greatest concern to analysts focusing on the mediating variables in the educational process, whether they be the grouping of youth by gross classification (e.g., special education) or the sorting of pupils into groups for instruction (see Good & Marshall, 1984; Oakes, 1985). As we have argued elsewhere, at the heart of the restructuring or transformational reform agenda underway throughout the United States are efforts to address the unequal distribution of outcomes by attacking the inequitable allocation of learning opportunities in schools (Murphy, 1991a, 1993b).

The increased prevalence of ethics in education can be traced to other sources as well. On the negative side, there is a growing awareness of the moral crisis in education (Purpel, 1989). On the positive side, there is an increasing recognition of the moral foundations of teaching (Bolin, 1989; Giroux, 1988) and of the value-laden dimensions of instruction and schooling (Goodlad, Soder, & Sirotnik, 1990). As the luster of scientific knowledge in education dims, the deeply ethical aspects of schooling—for so long masked by the purported objectivity of science—are becoming increasingly visible.

Not surprisingly, given the social and educational dynamics noted above, the moral dimensions of school administration are increasingly visible on the landscape of educational leadership. This phenomenon arises in part from the fact that educational administration is nested within these larger sets of forces. That is, school administration is responding to changes in its environment.

At the same time, however, some of the impetus for renewed interest in ethics is traceable to internal dynamics, namely, the shift from the behavioral science era to the dialectic era in educational administration. As we have discussed more fully elsewhere (Murphy, 1990a, 1992a), these major periods of change in the profession are usually marked by stringent critiques of the status quo and calls for alternative visions that often, paradoxically, focus on perspectives honored in eras historically preceding the one under attack. In the current era of transition, this trend has led to renewed attention to the practice dimensions of the profession—dimensions that were at the core of school leadership from 1900 to 1946 but were largely downplayed from 1946 to 1985. It has also rekindled interest in the moral underpinnings of leadership that, as we discussed earlier, were central to an understanding of administration prior to 1900, but that have since played a largely peripheral role in the profession.

Evidence of Change

Evidence for the growing importance of ethics in educational administration comes from a variety of sources.[9] First, as noted above, rigorous attacks on the privileged place of science and on the absence of attention to values in the profession reached a crescendo in the late 1980s and early 1990s (Murphy, 1990b, 1992a; Murphy & Hallinger, 1987). The following perspective from Greenfield (1988), one of the earliest and most thoughtful analysts of the lack of emphasis on the moral dimensions of leadership, is representative of the work in this area:

> For more than a quarter of a century, a fact-driven model of decision-making and rationality has dominated training programs for educational administrators. To the extent that these programs embrace technically oriented notions of administration, they offer less than they espouse. They miss the meaning of human action. (p. 154)

Second, thoughtful chroniclers of trends[10] in the profession such as Willower (1988) and Slater (1991)—quoted above—discern changes in educational administration consistent with this focus. As Culbertson (1988) puts it, "the concern for values has intensified" (p. 20).

Concomitantly, some of the most visible national reform reports in educational administration that have helped mark—and shape—the transition from the behavioral science to the dialectic era call for renewed attention to ethics and values throughout the profession.[11] For example, in its 1989 reform agenda, the National Policy Board for Educational Administration lists "moral and ethical dimensions of schooling" (p. 19) as one of seven curriculum strands to be emphasized in preparation programs.

At the same time, an expanding amount of scholarship is being devoted to the topic of ethics in educational administration.[12] The movement of the work of critical theorists and feminist scholars to center stage in the profession is both a cause and an effect of this phenomenon. A number of important new volumes focusing explicitly on ethics in school administration have also been published recently (see, for example, Barnett, McQuarrie & Norris, 1992; Beck, 1994a; Sergiovanni, 1992).

Finally, there is some preliminary evidence of heightened attention to ethics, especially as reflected in equity concerns in preparation programs throughout the country engaged in serious reform efforts (Murphy, in press a). For example, in an earlier review (Murphy, 1993c), we conclude that a conscious focus on values and ethics—what we label "extending the equity agenda" (p. 242)—is one of the key design principles of nine programs engaged in comprehensive efforts to improve the education of prospective school leaders.[13]

The evidence presented above on the reemergence of ethics in school administration is largely secondary—and, as reported in Notes 10-13, somewhat mixed—in nature. In the next chapter, by analyzing questionnaire data from 42 UCEA institutions, we provide a more direct test of the proposition that the role of ethics in preparation programs is being enhanced.

Notes

1. Shapiro and Smith-Rosenberg (1989) remind us that the deemphasis on ethics in educational administration preparation programs is part of the larger mosaic of a decline of ethics in the university curriculum in general.

2. It is important to acknowledge that our discussion here, as well as our analysis in Chapter 3, provides a macrolevel portrait of ethics in preparation programs. This tends to mask some of the specific ethical content that does find its way into programs for school leaders (Shapiro & Smith-Rosenberg, 1989).

3. Those interested in the history of preparation programs in school administration are directed to Campbell et al. (1987) and Murphy (1992a, 1993a).

4. For the Canadian analog of the Silver and Spuck study, see Miklos and Nixon (1978).

5. We use the terms weak and strong in this context in the following way. A strong, or more sensitive, test is one that allows any ethics related activity to show up in the assessment. Thus investigations that measure areas of emphasis or learning opportunities, or that unpack course syllabi to examine assigned reading (course content), would be examples of strong tests. An investigation of course titles in programs, on the other hand, would be a weak test, for ethics-related activities in courses not solely devoted to ethics would not be counted. Deducing the presence or absence of ethics in preparation programs by examining primary and secondary areas of faculty interest is also a weak (less sensitive) measure of ethics content.

6. We believe that Farquhar was overly generous in including this "effortless and incidental" group into the "are teaching ethics" category. This conception of ethics by osmosis is highly questionable. In reality, at the time Farquhar completed his study, the percentage of programs not dealing with ethics in any meaningful fashion was probably a lot closer to 90 than to 75.

7. As discussed earlier, this is a weak measure because the unit of analysis is "the student's official program of study," not "actual course content" (Norton & Levan, 1987, p. 21).

8. Although perhaps the weakest test for the place of ethics in educational administration preparation programs, data on area of primary faculty specialization collected by McCarthy, Kuh, Newell and Iacona (1988) and by Flanigan and Richardson (1992) also reveal that ethics/values is not a primary or secondary specialization in the profession. Specifically, none of the 15 specialty areas in the first study or 36 areas of expertise in the second investigation focuses on ethics.

9. One interesting, if somewhat crude, measure of the increasing popularity of ethics in education—at least in the academic

community—is the number of references to this topic in the index of the American Educational Research Association (AERA) annual program meeting. From 1986 to 1989, there were two or three references to ethics each year. In 1990 and 1991, there were four and five references respectively. In 1992 there were nine references, whereas in 1993 the number of references grew to eleven.

10. A careful reading of the history of educational administration leads us to be cautious about predicting trends in the profession, however (Murphy, 1992a, 1993a). There is a tendency to predict major changes—in curriculum, in instruction practices, etc.—on the basis of limited data. At the same time, given the information found in this section and in Chapter 3, we are comfortable with the claim that there is a rising trend toward an emphasis on ethics, morals, and values in school administration.

11. This conclusion is most true for the more academically oriented reform documents. Evidence of a renewed focus on ethics in the more practitioner-oriented reform reports is much less evident. For example, the National Commission for the Principalship (1990) has developed 21 performance domains of the principalship, only one of which—philosophical and cultural values—deals with ethics. Similarly, the National Association of Elementary School Principals (1990) has established 16 building blocks for the principalship, none of which deal directly with values or ethics. At the same time, however, it is worth noting that there is usually a gap of a decade or longer between the evolution of ideas in universities and the incorporation of those ideas into the world of practice (Beck & Murphy, 1993).

12. It is worth noting that Robert J. Starratt's piece on "Building an Ethical School" was selected as the best article in *Educational Administration Quarterly* in 1991.

13. As reported earlier, the evidence of this renewed focus on ethics is still far from conclusive, however. For example, in an earlier review of program activity in departments of educational administration, we (Murphy, 1991b) found little evidence that these "programs were spearheading the curriculum revisions called for by the National Policy Board for Educational Administration (NPBEA) in the moral and ethical dimensions of schooling" (p. 55). Similarly, in his review of five programs in the Danforth Foundation Principals' Program, Milstein's (1993) description, with one exception, provides few clues that would lead the reader to conclude that ethics and values are central elements

of program redesign. Finally, Pohland and Carlson (1993) found that only 12.5% of the 40 UCEA institutions in their sample offered educational administration-based courses in ethics and values in 1992-1993.

3

Ethics in Preparation
Programs Today

To everyone who proposes to have a good career, moral philosophy is indispensable.

Cicero from *De Officiis* (44 B.C.)

An Analysis of Survey Data From UCEA Institutions

During the fall of 1992, intrigued by our historical analyses of school administration—especially of preparation programs—and by what seemed to be an increased interest in ethics in administrative scholarship (e.g., Beck, 1992; Shapiro & Smith-Rosenberg, 1989; Slater, 1991; Starratt, 1991; Strike & Ternasky, 1993; Willower, 1988), we set out to replicate Farquhar's (1981) study on the status of ethics in UCEA institutions. Our original intent was to update the survey instrument from Farquhar's study. However, because it was impossible to locate a copy of that protocol, we developed our own. Professor Farquhar reviewed our survey instrument and indicated that it sought the same types of information for which he had looked nearly fifteen years earlier. Additionally, he offered several suggestions that helped us to expand the questions and refine the wording.

With the exception of one question, the survey contained open-ended inquiries that encouraged respondents to describe learning opportunities concerning ethics in the preparation programs. Surveys were sent to department chairs of the 50 (at that time) UCEA institutions.

In contrast to Farquhar's 37.5% response rate, 84% (42) of these questionnaires were returned to us.

The survey opened with our only forced choice question: "In your preparation program, to what extent is your department offering learning opportunities concerned with ethics?" Respondents were asked to choose between responses ranging from "not at all" to "a great deal." The breakdown of responses is offered in Table 1.

TABLE 1

Perceptions of Departmental Concern with Providing Learning Opportunities Dealing with Ethics

Response	Number of Institutions	Percentage
Not at all	1	2.5
Very little	16	38.0
Somewhat	21	50.0
A great deal	4	9.5
Totals	42	100.0

Because these are self-reports, answers to the first question offer only a weak assessment of the increased amount of attention to this topic. However, the lengthy answers provided by respondents to the open-ended questions that followed indicate that many institutions are making concerted efforts to address ethical issues in their curricular offerings.

As we reviewed the comments offered by department chairpersons (or, in a few cases, of other professors more clearly connected to ethics instruction), we were impressed by the recurrence of certain affirmations and assumptions. It seemed as if certain ideas—about ethics and educational administration, about the role of academic programs in this area, and about the ways this role might be fulfilled—were taking hold of the minds and hearts of professors and inspiring them to revise preparation programs consistent with their beliefs. In the following sections, we discuss themes that emerged from our analysis of professors' responses.

Assumptions About Ethics and Educational Administration

When Farquhar conducted his study 15 years ago, he interpreted the low response rate as an indicator of little interest in the whole subject of ethics in educational administration. If his assessment was accurate, it would be reasonable to infer from the high 84% response rate we received that this has changed and that the moral dimensions of leadership are, today, being given more serious consideration in academic circles.[1] As we unpacked the rationales offered as to why departments were or were not dealing with ethics, we found that respondents tended to see at least three links between this topic and educational administration.

Ethical Problems and School Leadership

Eight[2] respondents made explicit references to the fact that they, their colleagues, and students had come to believe that many problems facing administrators were either fundamentally ethical in nature or had important ethical dimensions to them. One chairperson indicated that, in his view, these problems were not sufficiently complex to merit special attention to ethics in his institution's course of study. However, for seven persons within this group, the treatment of ethics and values within preparation programs was important because it could assist leaders in coping effectively with these problems. The following comments are representative of those given by this group:

> School leaders have no professional training in this, but they have to deal with the problems every day.

> Administrators are faced with ethics issues all the time; how to approach them and giving some advanced thought to them will help them cope.

> Numbers of local school administrators have gotten into deep trouble by unethical actions.

For this group, the decision to pay attention to ethics within their preparation courses seemed to be a pragmatic one. Recognizing the practical need for administrators to be able to reason about these issues and to make judicious decisions, they suggested that their institutions were, in some ways, attempting to meet this need.

Increased Interest in Ethics and Trends in Scholarship and Policy

A second group of respondents provided slightly less practice-oriented rationales for their faculties' increasing willingness to examine ethical issues. Emphasizing that the Danforth Foundation and the University Council for Educational Administration had developed policy statements acknowledging ethics as an important arena for scholarship and discussion and that several well-known scholars (e.g., Foster, 1989; Sergiovanni, 1992; Strike et al., 1988) had also begun to articulate a theoretical basis for attention to moral leadership,[3] these individuals reported that their institutions were responding to this emphasis. Implicit in their statements is the conclusion that trends in academia are playing an important role in shaping their research and teaching interests. Thus, while they did not discount the importance of ethics for practicing educators, a concern with relevance to practice was not a dominant force shaping the treatment of ethics in their programs. Seven pointed out that "developing literature and interest in this subject," "emphasis in the field, reform statements, and practice," and a "general feeling of faculty members that there should be an [ethics] course" were prompting their faculties to consider adding ethical components to their programs. Five respondents who reported that their departments were already active in this area also credited emerging scholarship and reform policy—"reform literature and the influence of the national scene"—for inspiring efforts to incorporate discussions of ethics into existing courses and, in some instances, develop courses concentrating specifically on values and moral reasoning.

Educational Administration as a Fundamentally Ethical Endeavor

Interestingly, fourteen professors, in discussing reasons for an enhanced focus on ethics in their programs, wrote explicitly of their belief—and that of their colleagues—that educational leadership was, at its core, an ethical endeavor. These persons argued that any efforts to prepare individuals for this field must, therefore, attend to developing the ability of students to think and act in morally appropriate ways. The following three comments nicely summarize this perspective. One respondent wrote:

> Education is a moral enterprise. The leadership of schools (as with leadership of other such enterprises) requires a vision, an agenda for activities and outcomes, which tends to draw its strength from a basic set of beliefs. Ethical behavior is crucial in operationalizing that agenda or vision successfully.

Another chairperson, in offering the rationale for her institution's developing program noted:

> Education is very much a valuing process. It is expected to transmit values while being the focus of conflicting values within society. The administrator needs to understand how values affect his/her own behavior and the import of developing a personal set of values. Then the administrator is better able to lead the school in identifying and fostering ethical behavior in carrying out its missions.

A third professor reported:

> Administration is basically about making moral choices—routine choices are easy and require little or no ethical examination. The other ones engage the administrator in a major way.

This perception, expressed by fully one third of the respondents indicates a shift in thinking about leadership and about legitimate scholarship and teaching that can inform and develop leaders. Apparently the value-free preparation edifice of the social science era is crumbling (Murphy, 1992a). The belief that "the perfect administrator would be one who could perfectly separate fact from value" (Foster, 1984, p. 105) is no longer the normative assumption in many departments of educational administration.

Beliefs About the Role of Preparation
Programs in Developing Ethical Leaders

Not only do many professors of school administration comfortably espouse the idea that leadership within schools requires an ability to think and act ethically, they also, apparently, are endeavoring to translate their beliefs into curriculum in preparation programs—to encourage consideration of moral decision making and practice. In this section, we discuss three patterns in the data about the appropriate role of preparation programs in this area. The first is the belief that departments should not attempt to deal with ethics. Next, we focus on statements that suggest that certain faculties are beginning to discuss this issue and are considering the possibility of expanding their programs to address, in some way, the normative dimensions of leadership. We conclude with an examination of statements that indicate strong departmental support for including ethics—in some way—in the preparation experience.

Little Activity and Little Support for Ethics as a Part of the Curriculum

Of the 42 responses, only seven suggested that their departments were doing little (or nothing) in the area of ethics and that they had no plans to explore ways to incorporate this topic into their programmatic offerings. As we analyzed the various statements about why programs did not, should not, or would not incorporate ethics into the curriculum, we found only four that indicated that they did not see the need for learning opportunities in this area. Comments by two professors demonstrated that their departments had, in fact, made a conscious choice about the direction of their programs and that ethics was not a part of their plans. One underscored his institution's commitment to examining "psychological" not "philosophical" foundations. Another, describing colleagues as "utilitarians," claimed that her department's emphasis was "narrowly professional—concerned with what and how, not why." Others, although not entirely dismissing the importance of this body of knowledge, reported that they were not dealing with ethics primarily because there was no faculty interest and/or little room in the curriculum because of state-mandated requirements.

Discussions of More Direct Attention to Ethics

In contrast to those with no interest in administrative ethics, five respondents who did not rate their programs as being attuned to this issue reported that changes were possibly or "probably" going to occur that would bring this topic into a more central place. Four of these indicated that their institutions were making specific plans to do more with the moral dimensions of administration. One noted that, because of the "general feeling of faculty members that there should be a course," plans were being made. This professor requested information on activity in other universities so that these could be incorporated into the planning. Attaching a detailed set of plans (including likely syllabi), another chairperson reported that in the program that her institution was developing, "an ethics course as a part of the required core" had been proposed.

Faculty Support for Learning Opportunities on Ethics

Of the 26 professors who reported that their departments were somewhat or very active in this area, 19 wrote explicitly of widespread support among their faculties for such an effort. Their comments confirmed a point recorded earlier. Faculty members in school administration are beginning to view management as more than a technical, objective endeavor. They are considering ways to promote ethical thought and practice. One chairperson wrote:

> We are moving from a traditional manager in training orientation to a focus on the education of intellectual-moral-reflective leaders. Leadership is about courage, passion, and belief, and implementing these values to benefit children and the common good. At _____, we understand that a society in political, social, and economic transition needs to examine preparation programs driven by industrial values.

Another revealed how, after a period of "general faculty discussion and a process of program content development," a consensus regarding the importance of ethics was reached:

The department faculty concluded after a two plus year period of the development work on appropriate core and specialization content that ethics was *core* to all leadership preparation. (emphasis in the original)

Yet another affirmed that, in his department, "a small, but critical mass of university and school-based educators" demonstrated "strong commitments" to the following idea:

> Beliefs, values, and human interests are at the core of human activity. Leadership is the exercise of significant and responsible influence in human organizations with purpose and impact on the lives and welfare of human beings. Part (probably the most important part) of this responsibility, we believe, is to be able to cogently argue for, develop the warrants for, the core values/purposes of the educational organization. This is particularly important for compulsory public school in a pluralistic democracy.

Programmatic Responses to Increased Interest in Ethics

As chronicled in Chapter 2, representatives of seven institutions in Farquhar's (1981) study offered comments that "may be summarized as follows: ethics is an important topic and a neglected one; we don't do much or anything, specifically in this area at our institution" (p. 195). In contrast, eleven universities indicated that they were, in some way, attempting to address ethics in their educational administration programs. Discussing the various forms of these efforts, Farquhar concluded that five within this group seemed to embrace the position

> that matters related to ethics arise naturally in virtually all aspects of their preparation programs wherein the primary focus is on some other subjects; ethical concerns intrude during practical or clinical experience, during discussion of cases and simulations, and during regular courses through consideration of topics such as ethical responsibilities in the supervisory relationship, ethical uses of personal data, and ethical business relationship. *Thus, in these programs to the extent that ethics are*

treated it is done in an effortless and incidental way. (p. 196, emphasis added)

Farquhar noted that "two institutions ... reportedly endeavor *consciously to integrate* ethics into much of what they teach" (p. 196, emphasis added) and that four "have components within their administrator preparation programs that are *deliberately and distinctly focused* on the subject of ethics" (p. 196, emphasis added). The responses indicating a concerted effort to address ethics represented 33% of Farquhar's respondents and 12.5% of the population of UCEA institutions.

We found that department responses clustered into three general categories. In the first category, the program indicated no activity; whereas several reported incidental treatment. In the second category, a large number indicated that their faculties consciously integrated attention to ethical issues into various courses. Finally, in the third category, quite a few wrote of specific courses, some required and some elective, that dealt in a focused manner with administrative ethics and values. Below, we describe efforts that fall into each of these groups.

No or Little Activity in the Area of Ethics

As reported in Table 1, one respondent observed no activity in the area of ethics.[4] Of the 16 programs that noted little activity, seven reported that their institutions had no plans to change. Of the remaining nine, two noted courses outside the administrative curriculum in which students might get some exposure to ethics. The answers of others revealed that the prevailing view in this group was that an awareness of moral issues and of ways to think about such things was something that students would absorb in the course of their preparation. The words of one respondent nicely illustrate this view:

Ethics is presumed to be "picked up" as a "natural" outgrowth of instrumental studies—no one isolates it. There's no room in certification requirements.

The thinking underlying these apparently "effortless and incidental" approaches to ethics seems to have at least two threads running through it. One, hinted at in the words of the professor cited above, is the belief that an ethical leader is one who does her or his job effectively and that a preparatory program can best serve that end by focusing on the more instrumental dimensions of leadership. A second thread involves the idea that the ability to think and act in moral ways is something better caught than taught.

Conscious Efforts to Integrate Ethics Into the Curriculum

Twelve respondents described how, in their institutions, faculty were making a concerted effort to integrate ethics into other courses within their curricula. Many underscored the seriousness with which they were undertaking this challenge by outlining—in detail—the courses that had "strong ethics components," and several included syllabi that bore witness to the fact that texts and readings included works explicitly dealing with values and moral reasoning (see Chapter 4).

Interestingly, different institutions seemed to feel that ethics "fit" more appropriately into some courses than others. Four respondents specifically spoke of efforts to incorporate discussions of this topic into classes dealing with school law. Two, in turn, emphasized that they considered ethics to be a topic best addressed in philosophy of education courses. The largest number highlighted the importance of including consideration of ethics in courses designed to help practitioners make wise, judicious decisions. The words of one respondent nicely capture the thinking of the six professors who embraced this view:

> We work ethics into current courses in two ways (some courses more than others obviously). First, values in educational ad-ministration is a topic treated in our organization course—specifically, different approaches to values are considered and the theory[ies] behind valuations is/are examined. Second, in courses on decision making, specific choices between compet-ing values become the focus of the course. Efforts to examine optimum procedures for considering decision options in ways that reflect value choices are a major focus.

We are intrigued by the fact that the faculty of four institutions link ethical reasoning with legal reasoning and that six seem to view ethics as useful in that they supply principles to help guide administrative decisions. On the one hand, the reality that ten respondents seem to think of decision making as a critical—if not central—leadership task indicates that the ideas of those who sought to create a rational science of administration are still influential in academic circles. On the other hand, the fact that only one fourth of the respondents explicitly wrote of ethics as something of value *because they served the process of objectively weighing alternatives in problem solving* suggests that faculties may be beginning to view moral practice as something intrinsically valuable in school leaders.

Courses Focusing on Ethics, Values, and Moral Leadership

Respondents from seventeen institutions stated that they currently offer courses that specifically focus on administrative ethics.[5] One other chairperson noted that her department is revising its program "to incorporate moral/ethical dimensions into [its] core of seminars required at the doctoral level." Five professors expressly mentioned that these courses are required in at least one of their degree programs, and two stated that all students in all programs are expected to take courses in this area.

The courses—as described by respondents—vary in their approaches to ethics. Some seemed to embrace an emphasis discussed in the previous section in that they concentrate upon ways an awareness of ethical principles could enhance decision making and problem solving. One course, described as a required seminar for doctoral students, was entitled "Ethics and Educational Decision-Making." Taught by a professor specializing in policy studies, "the seminar examines ethics from a philosophical perspective but also includes a more current organizational studies examination of issues." In another institution, students taking "Analytical Studies in Educational Administration," "analyze ethical dilemmas and write their own professional code of ethics." Several noted that cases and/or actual incidents from practice provide a basis for discussions of ways administrators do and should deal with problems and complex situations.

Several other chairpersons described approaches that suggested that they were attempting to expand their focus beyond ethical problem solving. One stated:

There is an emphasis on creating a cohort of participants who operate as a learning community. This can only be done through bringing the mind, heart, and hand together. Thus, the ethics of human interaction is *lived* as we learn to value diversity as we create our version of a learning community of the future. (emphasis in original response)

Another wrote, "we have as one of six core areas—meaning" and indicated that "coursework and qualifying examination content in the area of ethics" were planned to address issues related to meanings attached to education and its leadership.

The facts that over one third of the institutions represented in this investigation have courses on ethics and that quite a few *require* students to take these in at least some degree programs further confirm our contention that shifts have occurred in the place of ethics in the field of educational administration. The reality that ethics and values are important enough to merit a place within our curricula demonstrates that, as a field, we are expanding our views of what constitutes good school leadership. This change may also indicate a certain confidence, a coming-of-age of educational administration as a profession and as a field of scholarly inquiry. As we have noted in earlier work (e.g., Beck, 1994a; Beck & Murphy, 1993; Murphy, 1992a), education has historically looked to other disciplines to define what constitutes good scholarship. Perhaps, in asserting that thinking and acting ethically are "a big part of the job of leadership" and that administrator preparation programs can and must support these activities, we are beginning to look at the challenges that face our particular field and develop ways to address these challenges systematically.[6]

Searching for an Explanation for Increased Attention to Ethics[7]

When we compare the findings gleaned from our survey data to Farquhar's (1981) results and to insights offered by others (e.g., Immegart & Burroughs, 1970; Norton & Levan, 1987; Silver & Spuck, 1978) whose research examined the place of ethics in preparation programs (see Chapter 2), we are struck by a rather dramatic shift in norms and practices. Once virtually ignored in academic programs, ethics and values are now receiving a fair amount of attention in departments of school administration. In our view, a number of factors—emanating from society, the educational field, and academia—have helped to spur this renewed interest in moral issues as they affect school leaders. In this section we discuss a number of these factors, including: demographic changes in the populations schools serve; increases in the numbers of women in leadership positions; changes in the political context of schooling; shifts in thinking about organizational structure; expanded notions of educational leadership; and increased attention to issues of practice within preparation programs.

Demographic Changes in the Populations Schools Serve

During the past quarter of a century we have witnessed an unparalleled number of changes in the circumstances of children and families schools are charged with serving. Minority enrollment in schools is rising as is the percentage of less advantaged youngsters (Carnegie Council on Adolescent Development, 1989; Quality Education for Minorities Project, 1990). There is a rapid increase in the number of non-English speaking students (Quality Education for Minorities Project, 1990). The traditional two-parent family, with one parent employed and the other at home to care for children, is an anomaly (Wagstaff & Gallagher, 1990). More than 20% of the children in the U.S. live in poverty (Kirst, McLaughlin, & Massell, 1989; Peterson, 1993). Accompanying and often exacerbated by these changes have been increases in youthful substance abuse and adolescent sexual activity (Carnegie Council on Adolescent Development, 1989; Wagstaff & Gallagher, 1990), dramatic increases in youthful violence, and significant achievement gaps between African American and Latino students and their White counterparts (Astuto, 1990).

These changes have, in effect, "unraveled" (Beck & Murphy, 1993, p. 181) traditional ways of thinking about education and its policies and structures. As a society, we are being forced to face the fact that many educational policies, structures, and systems all too often perpetuate inequities by advantaging, often unintentionally, those from privileged circumstances and disadvantaging others. In confronting this reality, many scholars and policymakers have come to believe that the school provides the best and most logical place to redress such injustice. Thus educational administrators in recent years have found themselves at the center of a number of social movements. As educators seek—at times frantically—to identify their role in the reconstruction of society and, at the same time, to discover functional ways to deal with rapidly changing populations of students, they find themselves confronted with fundamental questions about equity, freedom, character, justice, and the like. Thoughtful educators find themselves continually challenged to consider and defend their values and to ensure that behaviors, policies, and structures are consistent with espoused ethical commitments. Teachers and principals often bring these issues with them as they embark on professional training and, in a certain sense, force preparation programs to, in some way, acknowledge the importance of developing competence in moral reasoning. At the same time, ethical implications of these demographic changes are increasingly occupying the agendas of professors in departments of school administration. As they do, there is a natural tendency for professors to work their areas of interest into the curriculum.

Increased Numbers of Women in Leadership Positions and in Departments of Educational Administration

Demographic changes in another arena—the increasing number of women in administration—have also contributed to the willingness of academic programs to focus on value issues. As Ortiz and Marshall (1988; see also Schmuck, 1987) document, the number of women in administrative and academic positions has increased rather dramatically since midcentury.[8] These scholars, along with Gilligan (1982), Pitner (1987), Shakeshaft (1987), Noddings (1984, 1992), Astin and Leland (1991), Miller (1986), and Hampel (1988), emphasize that women often have a different orientation toward leadership goals and strategies. Reflecting on the research in this area, Sergiovanni (1992) describes the differences in the following way:

> Men tend to emphasize individual relationships, individual achievement, power as a source for controlling events and people, independence, authority, and set procedures. Women, by contrast, tend to emphasize successful relationships, affiliation, power as the means to achieve shared goals, connectedness, authenticity, and personal creativity. For most men, achievement has to do with the accomplishment of goals; for most women, achievement has to do with the building of connections between and among people. (p. 136)

This orientation toward the relational dimensions of education has built into it an overt concern with certain moral and ethical issues.

The influence of women in leadership practice is buttressed by the growing number of women holding faculty positions in departments of educational administration.[9] One manifestation of this trend can be seen in the expanding body of scholarship by and about women. Feminist critiques of traditional administrative theory and research and of the typical emphases of preparation programs (e.g., Eaker & Van Galen, 1993; Noddings, 1984; Shakeshaft, 1987; Shapiro & Smith-Rosenberg, 1989) have both spotlighted the impoverished nature of the ethics in such programs and acted as a clarion call for a broader orientation in our field. Similarly, recent works by several women (e.g., Beck, 1994a; Beck & Newman, 1992; Noddings, 1984, 1992, 1993) have provided suggestions regarding ways an ethic of care might influence administrative practice and policy. These scholars, both implicitly and explicitly, call for education that attends to the moral dimensions of leadership. Insofar as influential women see the development of caring school communities as an important goal, they are likely to view the values and moral perspectives that undergird this viewpoint as legitimate and important. Thus we contend that the rise in the number of women in the administrative field has helped to move ethics into a more central place in educational administration programs.[10]

Changes in the Political Context of Schooling

Paralleling the noted demographic shifts have been a variety of political changes—many of which direct policymakers, practicing educators, and academics to think deeply and seriously about values and actual and desirable ethical commitments. Campbell et al. (1987), Kluger (1977), and others point out that the 1954 *Brown v. Board of Education* decision forced educators to join judges, attorneys, lawmakers, and other government officials in discussing, debating, and—eventually—making decisions based upon conceptions of justice, equity, freedom, and equality. The very nature of these topics means that these interactions must raise questions about values and moral commitments and about ways to order actions so that they are consistent with espoused ethics.

Although the *Brown* decision focused on enhancing opportunities for those disenfranchised because of race, its impact on ethics, politics, and education was more global. As questions about equity, excellence, individual rights, and the public good were raised in various political arenas, educators found themselves forced to consider the intended and unintended impact of policies, programs, structures, curricula, and pedagogical strategies on women, the poor, the homeless, gays and lesbians, and others who might be considered underrepresented, if not marginalized. Issues such as sexuality education, the treatment of pregnant and parenting teens, tracking, and the like—once discussed in functional and instrumental terms—became imbued with moral significance (see e.g., Oakes, 1985; Vinovskis, 1988; Weinstein, 1989). Educators had to consider the values underlying their decisions and the impact of those values on human lives and relationships, on various cultural groups, and on society as a whole. They had to clarify—as never before—their understanding of education's purposes (Sergiovanni, 1992; Starratt, 1991; Vaill, 1984) and to defend their actions as they related to these purposes. Preparation programs, faced with demands for help in this area, now seem to be responding by developing more courses and experiences to assist prospective leaders in developing skills in moral reasoning.

Giroux (1988) points out another aspect of the political context that encouraged educational leaders to become more adept at thinking about ethics and values and in defending their positions from a moral perspective. He argues that the rise of "right-wing ideology" as a viable political position challenges persons in educational leadership positions to develop thoughtful rationales for their activities that respond to concerns raised by "various right-wing spokespersons, in and out of the government, [who] have become quite aggressive in pushing a program for schools to address and teach a particular set of moral values and virtues" (p. 42). Giroux argues that individuals within this conservative group have unashamedly based their arguments upon their commitment to certain ethical perspectives and, in so doing, have created a politically powerful agenda to guide educational practice. Giroux suggests that the actual and potential impact of the perspectives of this group on educational policy and practice serves as a kind of clarion call to all educators to become aware of their own values. Absent such awareness, he contends, educators, parents, policymakers, and students run the risk of being unwittingly shaped by ethical values they have not chosen. We suspect that the actual and potential impact of "the right-wing discourse on ethics" (p. 45) has helped to shape discussions of ethics in administrator preparation programs by pushing value-laden concepts to the center of educational debate and by forcing persons who disagree with neo-conservative ideology to develop their own understanding of the moral values driving their work.

Trends in Thinking About Organizational Structure

Prior to the early 1900s, schools tended to be organized as community centers, even as families, and many of the ethical principles associated with these entities seemed to permeate the thought and actions of teachers, parents, students, and others with an interest in education. With the advent of the industrial revolution, a new organizational model assumed a more prominent place. Bureaucracy—with its commitment to hierarchical lines of authority, clearly specified roles and responsibilities, and rational operating procedures that would result in effective, efficient, economical achievement of goals—became the preferred structure (Beck & Murphy, 1993; Callahan, 1962; Campbell et al., 1987). Although proponents of this model did not overtly embrace a particular ethical perspective, several were embedded in the principles underlying bureaucratic structures that, in turn, shaped administrator preparation programs (Callahan, 1962; Murphy, 1992b; Newlon, 1934). The commitment to objectivity, as we have noted earlier, implied that issues of value were irrelevant in organizations and that leaders of schools need not devote time to studying such phenomena (Greenfield, 1988). The concern with efficiency and economy, in a sense, took on almost religious proportions (see e.g., Callahan, 1962) and carried with it an unspoken commitment to utilitarian ethics. Further, this faith in hierarchical structures implied that persons at the top of organizational structures were, by virtue of knowledge and position, those best equipped to make decisions for those below them. This assumption has ethical implications because it entails beliefs about the values and rights of individuals and about the bases for those rights.

With the advent of "the information society of the twenty-first century" (Beck & Murphy, 1993, p. 184), a new form of organization is emerging to replace bureaucracy as the preferred model (Murphy, 1991a). This new model tends to be heterarchical and to emphasize a diffusion of responsibilities, shared rights, and collaboration. As this new model has become the focus of educational planning and policy (see e.g., Barth, 1990; Beck & Murphy, 1993; Clark & Meloy, 1989;

Sergiovanni, 1992, 1993a, 1993b), new ethical assumptions have been implicitly and explicitly introduced into these arenas. Noddings (1992) has articulately argued that an ethic of caring must become a central tenet in the organization of schooling, a view supported by Starratt (1991) who also suggests that ethics of critique and justice must play a pivotal role in the thinking and activity of educators. We assert that as scholars and practitioners have thoughtfully considered ways to create new types of organizations, they have had to think more directly about the ethical perspectives needed to sustain these forms. This, in our view, is another force that has contributed to the augmented focus on ethics in educational administration programs across the country.

Expanded Notions of Leadership

Hand in hand with changes in thinking about organizations have come changes in beliefs about the nature of leadership in these new structures. The movement away from bureaucracies in which those at the top control those below them and toward arrangements that emphasize collaboration, shared vision, consensus, and mutual empowerment requires new concepts of leadership. Writing about this phenomenon in noneducational settings, Scott and Rothman (1992) note a relationship among organizations that shun "needless layers of bureaucracy, . . . bloated management committees, . . . [and] unnecessary vicepresidents" (p. 209), corporate cultures in which moral commitments govern activities, and a belief that leaders should be "far-sighted people who visibly set their firms' moral tone" (p. 207). Others who have written on corporate leadership (e.g., Block, 1993; De Pree, 1989; Greenleaf, 1977; Koestenbaum, 1987, 1991; Weisbord, 1987) express similar sentiments in regard to the need for ethical leadership in modern organizations.

Many, writing on education, have also called for expanded notions of leadership (Murphy, 1992a).[11] For example, Sergiovanni (1992) contends that a major cause of "the failure of leadership" (p. 2) in schools and other organizations can be traced to two trends:

> First, we have come to view leadership as behavior rather than actions, as something psychological rather than spiritual, as having to do with persons rather than ideas. Second, in trying to understand what drives leadership, we have overemphasized

bureaucratic, psychological, and technical-rational authority, seriously neglecting professional and moral authority. (p. 3)

In an effort to remedy this, he presents a series of arguments to assist academics and practitioners in moving "the moral dimension in leadership away from the periphery and right to the center of inquiry, discussion, and practice" (p. 3).

Barth (1990), Beck (1994a), Beck and Murphy (1993), and others join with them in asserting that leaders must focus on the meaning and value of service and must embrace ethical perspectives consistent with commitments to seek the well-being of others, of the larger organization, and of society as a whole. Barth (1990), for instance, suggests that principals within a "community of leaders" (p. 142) might consider engaging in "servant leadership" (p. 143). In so doing, they will reckon with the ethical guidelines shaping their views of appropriate ways of interacting with others. Beck (1994a), in turn, proclaims the importance of a caring ethic for educational leaders, and Beck and Murphy (1993) insist that a principal, capable of leading schools into the twenty-first century, must embrace the role of "moral agent" (p. 194) among others.

Increased Attention to Issues of Practice in Preparation Programs

The recent decade has given rise to several important developments in administrative training programs (Murphy, 1992a, 1993c). One of these that, in our view, has contributed to the expanded attention to ethics we uncovered in this investigation is a growing concern for the practice dimensions of leadership. According to Murphy (1992a), this tendency has been linked, in large measure, to widespread disenchantment with the theory movement and its attendant beliefs that administration was a science that could be virtually perfected with enough attention to developing theories, testing them in a hypothetico-deductive manner, revising them, and continuing the process.

Noting that "the outcomes of the quest for a science of administration were considerably less robust than had been anticipated" (p. 69), Murphy (1992a), suggests that by the end of the 1970s, many had gone so far as to label the theory movement a failure. Throughout the late 1970s and 1980s, a number of scholars (e.g., Bridges, 1977; Greenfield, 1988; Mann, 1975; Murphy, 1989, 1990a, 1990c; Muth, 1989; Sergiovanni,

1984, 1989, 1991; Shakeshaft, 1987) engaged in a kind of postmortem of the efforts of previous years. Among other things, they concluded that two critical dimensions had been neglected in many university-based programs. These were a concern with problems of practice that inevitably bubbled up in "the protean cauldron in which the administrator knows himself to be" (Mann, 1975, p. 141) and an attention to "the moral dimensions" (Greenfield, 1988, p. 138) of leadership (see Murphy, 1992a).

For a number of reasons (not the least of which was the spate of criticisms aimed at schools and their leaders in the 1980s), a renewed interest in issues of practice and enhanced focus on clinical experience caught on rather quickly as faculty across the country began considering appropriate preparation experiences for aspiring leaders (see, e.g., Achilles, 1988; Bridges & Hallinger, 1991; Griffiths, Stout, & Forsyth, 1988; Murphy, 1992a; Murphy & Hallinger, 1987, 1992). Equally important for our purposes here, connections between the practice and ethical dimensions of schooling were being woven together in new ways. Our respondents seem to support this, for, as reported earlier, a large number of chairpersons indicated that problems in the field invariably had numerous ethical dimensions to them and that efforts to help leaders address the former meant that preparation programs must also deal with the latter. Thus we contend that the legitimizing of attention to practical issues has also been a factor in moving ethics and morals into a more central place in administrative programs.

We turn now to our analyses of course materials, especially syllabi, that can provide deeper insights into the nature of ethics in educational leadership preparation programs.

Notes

1. As we discussed briefly in Chapter 2, other evidence also exists to support this assertion. Chroniclers of trends in the professions (e.g., Culbertson, 1988; Murphy, 1993c; Slater, 1991; Willower, 1988) have noted an increased interest in ethics and values. Concomitantly, some of the highly visible national reform reports (e.g., National Policy Board for Educational Administration, 1989) call for renewed attention to these topics. Furthermore, an expanding amount of scholarship is being devoted to ethics in administration as evidenced by a number of new publications in this area.

2. Throughout this analysis, we mention the numbers of respondents whose comments buttress our identification of a particular theme. It is important to note that, at times, those answering our survey offered remarks that we have cited in more than one category.

3. Significantly, a number of scholars are engaging in parallel efforts to develop a theoretical basis for the moral dimensions of teaching. See, for example, the work of Bull (1993), Clark (1990), Fenstermacher (1990), Giroux (1988), Goodlad, Soder, and Sirotnik (1990), Grant (1993), Gross (1993), Jackson, Boostrom, and Hansen (1993), Macmillan (1993), Sichel (1993), Strike (1993), Strike and Soltis (1992), Thomas (1990).

4. Interestingly, several other respondents—when asked if they knew of other institutions that might be addressing the issues of ethics— referred us to another professor at this institution. Because this is a very large university, it is possible that some activity is occurring in this area but that the person answering our survey was unaware of it.

5. A number of universities that fell into the "somewhat" and "great deal" categories offered separate courses in ethics but also reported efforts to integrate this topic into other courses in their programs.

6. Recently, calls along these lines have been made by Miklos (1990) and by Sergiovanni (1992, 1993b).

7. In this chapter, we have discussed the results of our survey of 42 professors in UCEA institutions regarding their departments' programmatic treatment of issues related to ethics and values. In a similar vein, in the next chapter, we analyze the syllabi of courses in this area supplied by 17 respondents. As we conclude each of these reports, we have elected to spend some time reflecting on our findings in light of a larger body of scholarship. Here we concentrate upon possible explanations for the rather dramatic increase of interest in this area as evidenced by our data. We also comment, in a very general way, on other patterns related to various approaches to ethics. We do not, here, spend time considering specific curricular or pedagogic strategies (even if they were noted in the survey responses). In our view, this sort of discussion fits more logically into Chapter 4 where we examine, in some detail, texts, assignments, and teaching strategies.

8. It is important to point out that Ortiz and Marshall (1988) also stress that, although more women occupy positions in K-12 administration, in policy-making arenas, and on university faculties, they still represent only a small percentage of the total workforce in these areas.

9. McCarthy and her colleagues (1988) report that women hold about 11% of the faculty positions in departments of school administration, up from 3% in 1972.

10. Our argument is supported by the fact that, of the professors named by department chairs as teaching courses on ethics, five are women.

11. A number of scholars have begun to study the implementation of this emerging view of leadership in schools and school districts. See, for example, Murphy (in press c) and Murphy and Louis (1994).

4

Addressing Ethics
in Academic Courses

Although moral problems ought to be faced when they arise in the context of other courses, at the undergraduate or professional-school level, reliance should not be placed upon such sporadic encounters as a substitute for the availability of well-organized, full courses. No other serious subject is taught in the curriculum by what has been called the 'pervasive method,' and ethics ought not to be the outcast.

Daniel Callahan and Sissela Bok from *Ethics Teaching in Higher Education* (1980), p. 302

As noted in previous chapters, we asked professors responding to our survey to supply us with materials (including syllabi) that might give us deeper insight into their institutions' approaches to ethics. We were delighted to receive course syllabi from seventeen institutions. An analysis of these proved to be extremely useful in that they reinforced, clarified, and amplified survey responses. As we reflected on the range of courses dealing with ethics, we grew increasingly confident in our assertion that our field is, indeed, experiencing a surge of interest in the moral dimensions of leadership.

In addition to confirming this trend in preparation programs, our examination of the syllabi had two additional benefits. On a theoretical level, it provided clues about beliefs regarding the ethical challenges facing school leaders. At the same time, it offered insights into content of specific ideas and values that were considered relevant to administrators seeking to address those challenges. Thus examining course syllabi enabled us to gain a fuller picture of the assumptions within the academic arena about the art of administration and about the best and most appropriate ways to prepare school leaders. On a practical level, the syllabi sparked our thinking about ways we, as professors, might better assist our students in understanding the moral dimensions of their work, their own philosophical perspectives, and the way to order their professional activities so that they honor important ethical commitments.

It is our hope that readers will find this chapter on our colleagues' efforts to encourage ethical thought and practice both enlightening and practical. To that end, we order the discussion in the following manner. First, we begin with an overview of the syllabi, noting, in a very general way, some key features of the courses being offered. We then discuss, in greater detail, patterns and themes in the various programs. We review stated and implicit purposes of the courses, course content, and pedagogical strategies. In the concluding sections, we place these findings in the larger context of administrator preparation and specu-late upon the meaning of various teaching goals and activities. We attempt to situate these findings in the context of assertions made by us and others regarding the changing place of ethics in administrative preparation and practice. We also assess the ways these courses might mark changes in the ways we educate school leaders.

Overviewing Syllabi From UCEA Institutions

As noted above, representatives of seventeen universities—in ad-dition to responding to our survey—included syllabi or extensive descriptions of courses that reflected their institutions' efforts to ad-dress ethical issues. All four chairpersons who indicated that their departments were paying "a great deal of attention" to this area fell within this group. Ten who considered their programs to be "some-what" active provided syllabi as did three professors who noted that their institutions paid "very little" attention to ethics. Two respondents included several syllabi demonstrating the range of ways their depart-ments attempted to address this topic. Three others sent only a single syllabus but indicated that more than one course on this topic was offered in their educational administration program or in a related area (e.g., higher education, supervision).

Six department chairs stated that the syllabi they sent reflected a course that had only recently been developed in their department.

Offering comments such as "It's too early to tell the impact of our efforts in this area," three others implied that their ethics courses were relatively new. One, as noted above, sent a syllabus for a proposed course. In contrast, a single chair wrote that her department "historically" had "a strong orientation toward values education" and indicated that "Values and Ethics in Educational Leadership" has been required of all doctoral students since 1988.

Among the 17 chairs supplying information about specific courses, seven wrote specifically about the fact that ethics is now considered a part of their core program for administrators. Four of these respondents stated explicitly that a course dealing with ethics is required for doctoral students. The words of another implied that a newly instituted course, "Professional and Ethical Issues in Educational Administration," has recently become a requirement at his university. One chair reported that her department was in the process of revising its doctoral program and that the faculty was proposing that a course entitled "Ethics for Educators" be required. And the professor who sent syllabi for courses on "Organizational Development," "The Principalship," "School Law," "Problem Solving," and "Leadership" reported that all students are required to demonstrate mastery within the "domain of ethics and legal aspects" and that these five courses have substantial sections that deal with the ways norms, values, and moral commitments do and should guide leaders. Of the remaining ten respondents, eight noted that the ethics course at their institution was an elective.

Fifteen of the syllabi we received were the products of professors who, according to UCEA records, are faculty members within educational administration departments. Others teaching these courses are linked with departments devoted to educational philosophy, policy studies, and teacher preparation. As noted in Chapter 3, one third of the educational leadership professors teaching ethics courses are women.

Themes and Patterns of Ethics Courses in Educational Administration Programs

Analyzing syllabi developed by professors at different institutions was a demanding task. The documents came in many different forms. Some were quite extensive—outlining goals and objectives, readings, planned activities, and assignments in great detail. Brevity characterized others. For example, one simply noted the names of philosophers (e.g., Aristotle, Kant, Nozick, Rawls) whose works would be covered during the semester. However, most tended to articulate, in some way: the goals or objectives to be addressed; assigned readings; writing projects or other projects involving group work or oral presentations; and proposed evaluation strategies. Quite a few also discussed the pedagogical approaches that would be employed as the course unfolded.

In this analysis, therefore, we do not claim that we were working with comparable material, for we were not. Nonetheless, we were able to detect certain themes and patterns within and across the syllabi that suggest much about the ways ethical issues are being handled in many preparation programs. In this section, we unpack some of these under the following categories: (1) course purposes, (2) course content, and (3) pedagogical approaches.

Purposes Underlying Courses on Ethics

Professors attempting to articulate the purposes undergirding courses on ethics are entering into territory that, heretofore, has been relatively unexplored. As we noted in Chapter 1, the fact that there exists a range of beliefs about the nature and function of ethics in personal, professional, and social life is a particularly relevant challenge. In a similar vein, Daniel Callahan (1980) suggests that those involved in "the *teaching* of ethics"(p. 61, emphasis added) face an added difficulty, for he notes that even as the concept of "ethics" has multiple meanings so also does the idea of "teaching."

> The very phrase "the teaching of ethics" has a variety of connotations in our culture, and so for that matter does the term "ethics." One can never be certain just what people hear when they encounter the notion of "teaching ethics": for some, it means instructing people not to break the law or to abide by some legal or professional code; for others, it means an attempt to improve moral character or to instill certain virtues; for still others, it primarily means imparting special skills in the handling of moral argumentation. Moreover, clarity is by no means guaranteed by the standard method of simply stipulating one's own definitions or viewpoints. Someone who was once "taught ethics" by harsh and repressive methods of gross

indoctrination may have trouble understanding "the teaching of ethics" in any more benign sense, however carefully one may point out other possibilities. (p. 61)

Noting yet another challenge, May (1980) suggests that articulating reasons for teaching ethics to aspiring professionals is often problematic because "during the period of expanding professional education, the university. . . . largely disclaimed moral reflection and nurture as a part of its mission" (p. 207).

In spite of these challenges, most professors teaching courses on ethics wrote, in some detail in their syllabi, of their goals and objectives. These purposes tended to fall into one of three categories. Four[1] courses seemed to be cognitive in their orientation with the goal of "develop[ing] and nurtur[ing] ethical knowledge" in participants. Eight focused on issues—usually problems—arising in practice and encouraged participants to consider the ethical commitments and reasoning processes that might assist in addressing troubling situations. Devoting approximately one half of course time to ethical theories and one half to using concepts in addressing practical dilemmas, professors of six others indicated a desire to address both of these areas.

Courses Intended to Develop Students' Knowledge Base

Professors teaching the four courses with strong cognitive underpinnings focused on "covering various schools of philosophical ethics." One, whose course was intended to serve as "an introduction to the study of the place of values in education," took a distinctly historical approach. Beginning with "the Hellenistic Tradition and the Judeo-Christian Tradition," students taking this course traced the development of beliefs about morality in education, in the professions in general, and in society from ancient times to the present. Further, they were encouraged, through readings and written assignments, to consider the ways the "socio-cultural" roots of prevailing ethics continue to shape contemporary thinking.

In another course, a section devoted to ethics was embedded in a larger investigation of "major social and educational theories that have influenced educational policy formation and practice." The scholar responsible for this course organized it around schools of thought (e.g., "structuralism, positivism, romanticism, conservatism, Marxism, and other social movements such as social Darwinism." Class meetings at the beginning of the course focused on describing and analyzing these perspectives. Later meetings were then devoted to considering the "moral imperatives of leadership."

One professor—who described his course as "philosophical"—explored various schools of thought in a dialectical fashion. He noted:

> The course begins with the Platonic tradition of basing ethical decisions on dialectical reason. It continues with the major contrast in modern ethics between utilitarianism, which bases ethical decisions on the foreseen consequences, and Kantian ethics of the obligation of autonomous rational moral agents. Both of these views are contrasted with John Dewey's method of social inquiry into foreseeable consequences which, unlike utilitarianism, does not include a theory of duty. Further reading includes a survey of alternative approaches to utilitarian theory, including John Rawls' theory of justice, James Coleman's mediation between Rawls and his critic, Robert Nozick, and proposals for ethical decision-making contained in critical and hermeneutic literature.

The fourth course in this group is one taught by a professor described by the department chair as taking an "academic approach." The course covered various approaches to moral thought and reasoning.

Courses Focusing on Problems of Practice

As described on the syllabi we received, eight courses seemed to have as their objective the analysis of practical issues facing educational leaders. Ethical theories, principles, and reasoning strategies were studied in order to assist leaders in developing wise approaches to challenges, problems, and dilemmas. Within this group of eight, professors tended to stress one of three approaches to analyze the ethical dimensions of administrative work. Three structured their classes around very specific ethical dilemmas and asked students to consider principles that might prove useful in solving (or at least coping) with these. Three others ordered their classes around more general concerns (e.g., "discipline and punishment," "collection and use of information," "tenure," "declining international competitiveness," and "family stress") that were likely to affect most educational leaders. Again, these professors apparently took these topics as the starting point of discussions and asked students to contemplate the ways ethical commitments might inform or confound efforts to deal with them. In contrast, two courses seemed to spotlight, not problems, but rather examples of good practice. Professors leading these asked students to reflect upon the organizational contexts and personal and professional moral perspectives that would be likely to support fine "performance in a leadership situation."

The three courses that focused on specific cases or dilemmas all used *The Ethics of School Administration* by Strike, Haller, and Soltis (1988) as a text. According to the syllabi, the cases in this book were springboards to encourage students to consider principles and decision-making strategies. Interestingly, though, the professors responsible for these courses asked participants to analyze these cases in slightly different ways. One focused almost exclusively on the professional responsibilities of administrators and looked to "codes of ethics governing administration for K-12 schools" as guidelines for addressing textbook scenarios. Another seemed particularly interested in making students aware of their own beliefs and values. An early assignment invited students "to clarify their own values/ethics so they will have a clear basis for their administrative decision making and behavior" by writing a paper entitled "Who I Am and Where I'm Going." A later assignment involved investigation of cases in light of students' personal ethical commitments. A third professor, in turn, emphasized both personal and professional morality and asked her students to "compare and contrast one's own code of ethics with that of a professional code" and to confront the tensions inherent in this process.

As noted, other syllabi revealed that three professors, rather than analyzing specific dilemmas, elected to concentrate on more general issues facing administrators—issues that, invariably, had ethical dimensions to them. Two of these courses centered primarily on educational concerns. In one, students were confronted with issues affecting leaders in both K-12 and higher education administration such as "leadership, management, human resource development, research, instruction, students, admissions, athletics, finance, policy, discipline, affirmative action, and tenure." At another institution, the instructor identified a similar list of salient issues including:

- Grouping, tracking and labelling
- Discipline and punishment
- The collection and transmission of information about students and teachers
- Evaluation of teachers and students
- Determining the relevance of qualifications for positions
- The problem of affirmative action and "reverse discrimination"
- Equitable bases for school funding
- Freedom of speech and censorship

Another professor, in a course entitled "Crucial Issues in Education," looked, not to educational management issues, but rather to societal issues such as "decaying cities, declining international competitiveness, AIDS, [and] family stress" and encouraged students to consider their responses to the many pressures they confronted.

In the two other courses with a distinctively practical emphasis, professors eschewed a discussion of problems or dilemmas and, instead, underscored the relationship between excellent practice and the ethical commitments of administrators. In one, students were exposed to many manifestations of skillful leadership in education and business and were encouraged to think about the ways good leaders are shaped by carefully considered personal philosophies. In the other, "the major focus of the course is on each team of 4-5 students designing an ethical school." Explaining the rationale for this emphasis, the professor wrote:

> The rationale behind the course is that the administrator should concentrate on building a comprehensive ethical environment in the school, an environment that involves administrative decision making to be sure, but one that involves the whole community. . . . I believe that students are forced to broaden and deepen their understanding of an ethical world view by working toward institutional transformation.

Courses Focusing on Both Theories and Practice

All of the courses discussed above certainly blend, to some degree, attention both to ethical theories and to issues of practice. They, however, tend to focus quite heavily on one dimension or the other. The six we discuss here were portrayed in terms that indicated a conscious effort on the part of professors to devote approximately equal amounts of time to developing students' knowledge of ethical theories, principles, and reasoning strategies and to investigating ways these might be useful in solving day-to-day problems.

The words of one instructor nicely illustrate the dual emphases of the courses in this group. He wrote:

> There are two major objectives in this course: to examine the central features of ethical theory and to consider problems in education involving ethical considerations. The first part examines philosophical views of ethics, morality, and education. The second part focuses on fundamental ethical issues and dilemmas. Topics covered include: lying, equality, liberty, punishment, authority, and justice.

In order to achieve these purposes, this instructor apparently spent part of each class meeting discussing ethical theories or principles (e.g., "Ethical Relativism," "Justification and Truth," "Relativity and Diversity in Morals") and part inviting analyses of cases.

Another course took a slightly different approach. Early in the semester, sessions followed a fairly traditional academic format with lectures and discussions on various philosophical perspectives and theories of moral development. Beginning with a consideration of "historical perspectives on ethics as a field of study," students were exposed to the writings of a number of scholars in order "to acquaint the student with the literature of ethics and values." Later classes then centered on moral dilemmas with writing assignments aimed at students' examining the meaning of philosophical constructs for their lives and work.

Course Content

In a thoughtful discussion of ethics in preservice programs for teachers, Barry Bull (1993) describes a resurgence of interest in addressing ethical issues in teacher preparation—a resurgence that he attributes to "a renewed conviction that teaching itself has an inherent moral dimension" (p. 70). He points out, however, that the ideas fueling "our current enthusiasm" (p. 70) offer little in the way of guidance to persons seeking to develop courses in this area. Bull discusses several problems facing those undertaking this task. One difficulty lies in the fact that there is little agreement regarding the scope, nature, and guiding perspectives for ethics classes. Thus professors teaching in this area must select the content they will cover, recognizing that embedded in their decisions to include certain materials and omit others are a host of contentious ideological positions. Another challenge is linked to the great variance in possible approaches to teaching on and about moral issues. After reviewing several of these—all of which have advantages and shortcomings—Bull observes that, at this point, we have "many more questions than answers" (p. 81) in regard to approaches for teaching in this arena. He concludes by noting that "the task of defining a fully satisfactory approach to [course] content is one that will take real moral and creative energies" (p. 82).

In this section, we turn our attention to the ways respondents have addressed these challenges and discuss course content as manifested in reading assignments. In the next section, we examine the pedagogical strategies being used in ethics classes in departments of educational administration. In regard to course content, we discuss four trends in the syllabi we examined: (1) written cases and dilemmas; (2) readings from outside of education; (3) readings focusing on professional ethics; and (4) readings discussing specific ethical principles or issues.

Course Content: Cases

Written cases or stories with embedded dilemmas provided a large portion of the reading material for eight of the courses we examined. Interestingly, each of these courses utilized at least one of two texts. Two professors assigned Kenneth Strike and Jonas Soltis's *The Ethics of Teaching* (1992); four chose Strike, Haller, and Soltis's *The Ethics of School Administration* (1988); and two courses required both of these books. In six courses, these works were part of an array of assigned readings. Typically in these, most class sessions would be devoted to a discussion of a particular concept (e.g., liberty, individualism, justice, utilitarianism), and appropriate cases would be used to allow students to wrestle with the practical implications of being guided by some principle or ideal. In contrast, two classes revolved around cases or dilemmas. In one, the Strike, Haller, and Soltis's (1988) work was the only text. In the other, an additional book supplemented the discussions and definitions offered by Strike and his colleagues. In both of these courses, the primary emphasis seemed to be on developing students' skills in reasoning and problem solving, whereas in the six others in this group, there seemed to be some concern with students' gaining an academic knowledge of ethical theory.

Course Content: Readings Outside the Educational Field

Twelve syllabi revealed that professors offering courses on administrative ethics were drawing on literature outside the field of education. Pulled from a number of disciplines, these particular readings varied widely, although all fell under an expanded conception of the humanities. The largest number came from philosophy and sociology. Works by Bellah, Madsen, Sullivan, Swidler, and Tipton (1985, 1991) appeared on a number of syllabi as did books and articles by philosophers (e.g., Dewey, 1916, 1963; Rorty, 1982). In one course, students were assigned portions of Carol Gilligan's *In a Different Voice* (1982) as a part of a section on various "approaches to moral and ethical reasoning," and in another, psychological literature that addressed various cognitive and interpersonal styles was used to invite students to consider the forces shaping their own decision-making patterns and preferences.

Three courses used literature as a springboard for reflection and discussion. In one, students were asked to consider the poetry of Walt Whitman in order to understand an individualistic perspective and its attendant ethics and values. In another, Plato's *Protagorus* (1976) was assigned in conjunction with the first course topic "What is ethics?" This text provided exposure to "the Platonic tradition of basing ethical decisions on dialectical reason," an approach that the professor endorsed as students attempted to understand, compare, and synthesize various ethical perspectives. In a third course, one novel—Kazuo Ishiguro's *The Remains of the Day* (1989)—was assigned to encourage students to consider "the lifelong undertaking of understanding one's self," whereas a second novel—Milan Fust's *The Story of My Wife* (1957/ 1989)—was recommended to spark further reflection on self, others, and moral ways of acting and interacting.

Course Content: Readings on Professionalism and Professional Ethics

As noted in the preceding paragraphs, twelve courses had assigned readings that were not explicitly educational. Some of these concentrated upon the notion of professional ethics. Students were asked to consider their moral commitments in light of their responsibilities as professional educational leaders. Readings highlighting these issues were quite varied. In a number of the courses we reviewed, the topic of professionalism was examined through works such as Callahan's *Ethical Issues in Professional Life* (1988), Camenisch's *Grounding Professional Ethics in Pluralistic Society* (1983), and Kultgen's *Ethics and Professionalism* (1988). Three courses delved into specific professions and their respective moral codes and included readings on ethics in law, business, and medicine. Students were asked to consider the links between the nature of work in these areas, the types of dilemmas professionals encounter, and the various ethical guidelines that have (or should be) established for guidance and protection.

Course Content: Readings on Specific Ethical Issues

Another interesting pattern was evident in the reading assignments of seven courses we examined. In addition to readings *about* ethics and *about* professionalism, professors leading these classes incorporated what we have labeled "professional issues" reading assignments. Frequently, these would require that students examine articles offering opposing perspectives on issues likely to arise in the workplace, such as truth-telling, whistle-blowing, or affirmative action. When this strategy was used, professors seemed to be concentrating less on the specific issues and more on the "value-conflicts or tensions" exemplified by the competing views in the assignments. One professor offered an especially articulate explanation of her rationale for asking students in professional programs to read such works. She wrote:

> Often values conflict or are in tension with one another. Sometimes value-tensions are explicit. Most of the time, they're implicit and unexamined by the author or speaker. Unless values are examined for possible conflicts, the policies and

reforms we adopt for education may end up doing exactly the opposite of what we want to achieve.

She then explained that her choice regarding readings was guided, in part, by her intention to represent two types of value-conflicts: ones in which "two 'goods' compete with each other" and ones in which "a 'pull' of opposing tendencies with one value" has a tendency to muddle thinking. Her hope was that she could assist aspiring educators in responding to ambiguous issues in a manner consistent with high professional standards.

Pedagogical Approaches

As we consider pedagogical strategies, we look first at the various deductive approaches represented in our sample and then examine more inductive and reflective teaching strategies.

Teaching Strategies: Deductive Approaches

Five of the syllabi we analyzed revealed that professors tended to teach in a rather deductive fashion. In one, for instance, readings, lectures, and discussions provided a historical overview of influential ethical theory, and students were expected to master important points as a part of developing their knowledge base. Worthy of note is the fact that the relevance and applicability of ideas were not neglected in this course. However, the approach to discovering relevance involved knowing the theories first and then finding situations that might illustrate or be informed by them.

The description of a writing assignment in a second class provides another example of this deductive approach. After studying concepts related to professionalism and professional ethics, students were asked "to develop a paper on the ethical and professionalism issues confronting leaders in educational organizations, [a] paper [that] will provide students with an opportunity to apply the concepts introduced in this course to situations in the professional workplace." Again, we see students learning various theories and demonstrating that they had a mastery of these on midterm and final examinations. Then, drawing upon this body of knowledge, they were asked to deduce ways such ideas might influence their work.

Teaching Strategies: Inductive Approaches

In contrast, instructors in eight courses employed decidedly inductive teaching strategies. Clearly articulating this approach, one professor stated that students would:

a. search out assigned background information related to ethical practices,
b. analyze cases related to ethical behavior of K-12 school administrators, and
c. present and defend the analysis of cases before the class.

In this course, cases, actual and fictional, formed the heart of the class. Confronted with these, students were asked to uncover ethical theories, principles, and decision-making approaches as they applied to the situation under consideration. Although the syllabi suggested that the professor presented, in a general way, some ideas about important issues, the thrust of this class was on students "discovering" concepts and ideas.

In another course, a set of complex questions (e.g., "Can a 'vision' be identified which characterizes America?" "Whose values inform public schooling?" and "How do educational policies and programs embody, further, or suppress social values and moral commitments?") provided the centerpiece of the course. Class activities and assignments were designed to prompt students' grappling with these questions and considering the implications of their answers for actual work in schools.

Teaching Strategies: "Mixed" Approaches

Three courses used what might be described as a mixed approach. In these, students were exposed to a defined knowledge base. One professor emphasized the importance of students examining "traditional ethics and alternative forms of moral development" and apparently presented these in a fairly traditional lecture and discussion fashion. Another expressly stated that one goal of his class was to have students "develop a knowledge base in various ethical issues." A third instructor described one of his objectives as follows: "to acquaint students with literature of ethics and values." In each case, however, students were asked to engage issues inductively as they chronicled their own ethical dilemmas and problems. Analysis often involved drawing upon class notes. Students were also encouraged to go beyond material covered in class—to seek other principles or sources of guidance and to allow this experience to assist them in critiquing literature on ethics.

Teaching Strategies: Reflective Approaches

A fourth pattern emerged in a number of classes. This was the tendency to encourage students to reflect upon their personal beliefs— "to look deeply within [themselves], to ask [themselves] basic critical questions, and to struggle with priorities among values [they] hold." With only one exception, the courses in which contemplation and self-awareness were emphasized were those that employed a more inductive approach to the content. Professors in these courses used several devices to encourage reflection. One, for example, asked each student "to keep a diary/log of the ethical issues, and/or decisions, problems, or concerns with ethical implications that confront you as an administrator (or confront an administrator you can watch closely) for *one* week." This instructor also required three personal essays that nicely demonstrated her reflective emphasis. In one, students were called upon to espouse their personal values and ethical principles, explain why they chose these, and "consider how [they] came to hold them." In the second, students were expected to confront their own behaviors and consider what ethics or values actually "*direct* and/or *guide* and/or most *influence*" them. And in the third, they were asked to reflect on the links between their espoused values and those that influenced and drove their practice.

Another professor assigned the writing of personal and professional ethical codes to encourage students to contemplate possible conflicts that might occur should these two sets of beliefs collide. One invited students to write him letters during the semester in which they could contemplate insights and express questions or frustrations. In yet another course, the instructor asked members of his class to develop a case in which "a leader is confronted with a dilemma where a solution will not resolve" it. As one part of this assignment, students were asked to confront their reactions to these apparently insoluble problems, for the professor was concerned that students probe deeply into the complex nature of ethical commitments and avoid easy, "quick-fix" strategies for addressing dilemmas.

Examining Findings in a Larger Context
Interpreting Beliefs About Purposes of Courses on Ethics

In *Ethics Teaching and Higher Education* (Callahan, 1980), Daniel Callahan suggests that anyone involved in "the teaching of ethics" (p. 61) must seek to address three "obvious questions":

1. Why should one want to undertake such a venture in the first place?
2. What could or should be accomplished by such teaching?
3. What is the nature of the subjective matter, ethics? (p. 62)

Callahan goes on to point out that the obviousness of these questions does not mean that they are easily or quickly answered. Acknowledging a "range and multiplicity of settings and contexts for the teaching of ethics" (p. 61) and the reality that "many disagreements" (p. 62) characterize discussions in this area, he notes that those undertaking responsibility for ethics courses are demonstrating a certain amount of courage as they engage these questions.

The statements of purpose on the syllabi we examined, especially when read in conjunction with survey responses, suggest that faculty members in departments of educational administration—even those who believe ethics is important for the practice of leadership—have not reached consensus on answers to Callahan's questions. We found indications that some would answer the "why" question by saying that ethics is a necessary topic to help administrators cope wisely and legally with the complex dilemmas they face. We uncovered signs that a number believe this topic is important as educational leaders seek to receive recognition as true professionals. Those embracing this perspective seemed to agree with May (1980) that professions are defined in part by their adherence to a code of conduct and to the moral commitments underlying this adherence. We also, though, detected clues that many professors and the departments they represent are starting to ask hard questions about the meaning of leadership and of education and, in their efforts to answer these, are beginning to reckon with the centrality of morality to endeavors that support, direct, and shape lives.

Similarly, course descriptions suggest that professors and departments define "ethics"—at least as they relate to the preparation of school administrators—in several ways. In Chapter 1, we wrote of six different ways of understanding this concept and noted that professional ethics can be functionally equated with various decision-making, problem-solving principles such as those found in philosophical constructs, legal principles, or professional codes of conduct. We also argued that ethics can be viewed, not primarily as a set of ideas, but rather as a more holistic concept that affects one's very being. In this regard, we explored different variations on this idea that stress ways of seeing, functioning politically and societally, and relating to self and others. Most of the syllabi in this sample focused on ethics as problem-solving principles, derived from a range of sources. Several, however, seemed to be moving toward linking awareness of various principles with "moral sensitivity," integrity in linking actions with espoused commitments, and the like.

Regardless of approach, the stated and implicit purposes of these courses suggest that some faculty and departments are making concerted efforts to move toward developing new programs in order to meet the important challenge of providing "leadership to communities so that children and young adults are well-educated in the deepest sense of that word" (Murphy, 1992a, p. 139). This process, in our view, means embracing four distinct goals: "helping prospective leaders to become moral agents, educators, inquirers, and students of the human condition" (p. 140). The syllabi we reviewed indicated that these goals—especially the first and last—have attained a certain legitimacy in some of our institutions.

Interpreting Patterns in Regard to Course Content and Teaching Strategies

As noted previously, many of the courses we examined represent relatively new additions to departmental curricula. Professors developing these courses are proceeding without much in the way of agreement on knowledge bases, tested teaching strategies, and commonly used texts to inform them. In so doing, they are stretching in a variety of directions. Even those who articulate similar purposes often attempt to achieve these goals utilizing quite different types of reading and writing assignments and teaching strategies. In our view, this variety represents an important and positive shift in our understanding of leadership preparation—even as the renewed interest in ethics foreshadows a revision in our assumptions about leaders' roles and responsibilities.

Critiques of traditional leadership preparation programs (Culbertson & Farquhar, 1970; Erlandson & Witters-Churchill, 1988; Farquhar & Piele, 1972; Hall & McIntyre, 1957; Mulkeen & Tetenbaum, 1990; Murphy & Hallinger, 1987; Murphy, 1992a; Silver, 1978) point out several important deficiencies. One of these, described by Griffiths (1988) as "perhaps the single most destructive trend affecting professional preparation during the last thirty years" (p. 299) is "the attempt by professional educators to develop a pseudo arts and science degree" (p. 18). One characteristic of this type of degree is a fairly monolithic approach in terms of program content and approaches. As Campbell (1981) and others have noted, the arts and science model is based upon study of the disciplines, something that presupposes agreement about the knowledge bases embedded in these various academic areas. And, as the critics noted above have reported, the teaching strategies in professional programs patterned after their arts and science counterparts have tended to "be lecture and discussion in a classroom setting based on the use of a textbook" (Mulkeen & Tetenbaum, 1990, p. 20; see also Erlandson & Witters-Churchill, 1988). Although some efforts have been made "to infuse reality-oriented instructional strategies into preparation programs, the change has hardly been revolutionary and the use of innovative pedagogical methods is not prevalent" (Murphy, 1992a, p. 103). In the multiplicity of readings and texts in the courses we examined and the varied instructional methods being utilized, we see hints of movement in a different direction.

The Use of Cases as an Emerging Pattern

The use of case dilemmas as course content and of case analysis as a central teaching strategy, practices we discovered in a large number of courses, bear witness to several emerging trends. These include: a growing concern with developing skills in moral reasoning; a belief that these skills should be practiced in simulated situations; an acceptance of the idea that many problems facing leaders do not lend themselves to neat, easily discovered solutions; and an interest in equipping prospective leaders to discuss moral issues and present thoughtful rationales for positions and decisions.

Several scholars have provided articulate discussions of links between case analysis and the development of competence in moral reasoning. Strike (1993), for instance, argues that students, when given extended opportunities to confront and work with ethical dilemmas, tend to grow in their ability to perceive moral issues embedded in these situations, learn to recognize the implications of various solutions, and become increasingly adept at discussing these with their colleagues. In the same vein, Strike, Haller, and Soltis (1988) and Strike and Soltis (1992) claim that cases provide an appropriate and useful venue to increase students' awareness of moral principles and enable them to develop skills in reasoning based upon these principles.

Culbertson (1964), Gregg (1969), and Griffiths (1959), are among those who assert that the application of theoretical constructs to actual leadership activities is greatly facilitated when professors utilize "simulated situations [to] involve the student emotionally as well as intellectually and also [to] help bridge the gap between theory and practice" (Gregg, 1969, p. 998). Murphy (1992a), Murphy and Hallinger (1987), Pitner (1987) and others concur with these views and hail the use of cases as a move away from "the sterility of 'classroom bound' instruction" (Wynn, 1972, p. 10) toward more reality-based curricula.

As professors lead courses focusing on the realities of administrative life and the types of ethical dilemmas that confront school leaders on an almost daily basis, they must acknowledge what Derek Bok (1982) has called "the limits of reason" (p. 128). They must accept the reality that easy, neat resolutions of moral tensions are elusive and that some problems are, perhaps, intractable (Cuban, 1992). Strike (1993) contends that cases are especially well-suited for teaching courses addressing such situations. He notes that a primary purpose of cases is to expose students to situations wherein moral principles or values collide. As they struggle with their peers over approaches to these dilemmas, students are forced to resist movement toward readily accessible strategies based solely upon utility or upon some "intuitive sense of right and wrong" (p. 107) and to develop "dialogical competence in the public moral language" (p. 107). For Strike, the process of developing such competence is inherently "dialectical [with] constant motion between . . . various levels of thought" (p. 110). Prompted by cases, students learn to consider and balance multiple viewpoints and reckon with the fact that they must function in environments where "there is not always one right answer or one best choice" (p. 116).

For Strike (1993), the pursuit of such reasoning skills in ambiguous and complex situations should assist students in making "principled moral decisions" (p. 116) that, in his view, are appropriate for educational professionals. He suggests that these decisions reflect "public moral principles that would be accepted after open and undominated discussion by reasonable individuals with potentially conflicting interests and outlooks" (p. 116). Strike is quick to point out that such decisions are necessary if administrators are to manage values conflicts, acknowledge the validity of multiple viewpoints, and make decisions that move them and their schools beyond a particular set of problematic circumstances. Echoing points made by Sergiovanni (1987), Murphy (1992a), Beck (1994a), and others, he contends that the ability to engage others in discussions of these issues, lead in a decision-making process, and provide a public rationale for positions and decisions is central to administrative success.

The Emphasis on Reflection as an Indicator of an Emerging Trend

The concern with reflection on one's personal and professional beliefs and actions, another trend in the courses within our sample, suggests that at least two relatively new patterns may be emerging in leadership preparation programs. First, a reflective emphasis indicates a possible shift away from a Weberian understanding of organizations as rational bureaucracies toward the phenomenological perspective advocated by T. B. Greenfield (e.g., 1988, 1991). Second, this approach suggests a growing faith in the notion of experiential learning (Dewey, 1938) or situated cognition (Brown, Collins, & Duguid, 1989) in preparation programs (Hallinger, Leithwood, & Murphy, 1993; Prestine & LeGrand, 1990).

The connection between a phenomenological understanding of organizations and the encouragement of reflection in preparation programs has been discussed by Osterman and Kottkamp (1993). Noting that a bureaucratic view of organization has, in the past, shaped educational scholarship and practice, these authors see links between the norms and beliefs inherent in this way of thinking and the content and delivery of preparation programs. Indeed, they assert that the belief that organizations function best as hierarchies with clearly defined roles and responsibilities and with decision-making power vested in the top bureaucratic levels is related to the assumption that organizational leaders can (and should) be prepared by exposure to discreet bodies of knowledge determined by superordinates in state credentialing agencies and research universities. When reflection is introduced as an integral and legitimate part of the preparation experience, Osterman and Kottkamp contend that the top-down assumptions of bureaucracies and traditional preparation programs yield to a "people-in-the-center" (p. 6) view of organizations.[2] This concept hinges upon the belief that mandates and policies issued from the top levels of the organization are not capable of affecting change. It also presupposes that theories and research conclusions discovered in the academic arena and communicated via journals, books, and articles are ineffective in transforming practice. Instead, it contends that organizations change as those inhabiting them alter their own norms, beliefs, ethical commitments, problem-solving strategies, and behaviors. Osterman and Kottkamp (1993), building upon the work of Schon (1983, 1987) and others, assert that reflection is pivotal in encouraging changes in "traditionally accepted behavior patterns or 'behavioral regularities' (Sarason, 1990) that lie below the surface of our awareness" (p. 6).

Advocates of reflection contend that it encourages change by providing opportunities for individuals to consider their own behaviors in light of their espoused theories and commitments. Thus it takes as a starting point personal experiences and assumes that these provide a foundation for learning. In doing this, a reflective approach differs from one that is grounded on "conceptual frameworks and theory-based empirical evidence" (Silver, 1982, p. 52) as the necessary material for productive preparation experiences. Osterman and Kottkamp (1993) contend that the belief that experiences are good fodder for intellectual growth and personal and professional development is one with a long tradition. "Experiential learning theorists, including Dewey, Lewin, and Piaget, maintain that learning is most effective, most likely to lead to behavioral change, when it begins with experience" (p. 20). They, joined by Knowles (1990), Levine, Barth, and Haskins (1987), Murphy and Hallinger (1987), Pitner (1987), and others, also point out that grounding learning in the realities of students' lives is quite consistent with insights derived from the growing body of research on adult learning. Because reflection invites—and, indeed, often depends upon— a consideration of actual experience, its use as a pedagogical strategy suggests that the knowledge of practice is, in some settings, being considered a valid and important part of the preparation of educational leaders.

The Use of the Humanities as Evidence of a Possible Resurgence of an Earlier Pattern

In his helpful overview of the development of administrative scholarship, Culbertson (1988) notes that the earliest efforts to prepare school leaders focused on exposure to classical philosophy, the Bible, and similar works. With the advent of the industrial revolution, however, persons interested in equipping principals and superintendents turned away from philosophy, history, and literature and began to look to "industrial and social science research into human behavior in the workplace and elsewhere" (Campbell et al., 1987, p. 19) to provide the knowledge and skills aspiring leaders would need (Callahan & Button, 1964; Cooper & Boyd, 1987). For the most part, the faith that theory-driven research can provide the answers to the problems administrators face and the subsequent inclusion of heavy doses of readings about techniques that purportedly demonstrate this have continued to characterize preparation programs. However, through the years a small number of scholars (see especially Brieschke, 1990; Farquhar, 1968; Miklos, 1977-1978; Popper, 1990) have persisted in asserting that the humanities provide critical and necessary learning experiences and should be a part of professional development efforts.

Brieschke (1990) contends that reading fiction enables persons to imaginatively enter the worlds of others, see the world through their eyes, and consider their concerns and values. Such skills, she suggests, are central to good administrative practice. Popper (1990) offers similar views. Asserting that leaders must "shift from a reliance on a coercive capacity in administrative control to a reliance on leadership influence" (p. 5), he insists that doing this "is a skill derived from multiple insights into the human situation" (p. 5). For Popper, contemplation of the humanities, of novels, plays, poetry, and the like, assist in the development of "empathic insight" (p. 6), for they move persons to understand others in an intuitive and personal way. Leaders possessing this "aesthetic enlightenment" (p. 7) are, in his view, better able "to relate with a heightened empathy to the significant other in a professional encounter" (p. 7). Regardless of the moral value of being able to function in this way, Popper argues that empathic skill can be of considerable instrumental value to administrative process in the all-important leadership task of fusing informal organization with formal organization. When the tactical objective is to keep in low profile the power dimension of administrative office and to maximize idiographic opportunities to raise system efficiency, then empathy-based perceptions of formal organization are indeed an asset to administrative leadership. (p. 7)

Thus Popper claims that even the most instrumental programs should include readings from the humanities as a part of the preparatory experience.

As we noted, a few of the courses we reviewed devoted a fair amount of time to consideration of poetry and novels, and classical philosophy, and other items that might fall into the humanities category. Although this may not signal a major shift in our programs, it does indicate an ongoing openness to nonscientific, nontechnical knowledge. Coupled with the other changes we have discussed in this and the preceding chapter, we suspect that more novels, poems, and plays will appear on various reading lists.

Concluding Thoughts

The diverse approaches to ethics in educational administration that were described by survey respondents and revealed more fully in course syllabi reveal that departments are engaging in conversations about the meaning of moral leadership and the most appropriate ways to encourage it. As we stated, we applaud the fact that such discussions are occurring. We also recognize, though, that dialogues about ethics can turn rather quickly into diatribes or debates. In the final chapter, we propose a framework for grounding conversations about ethics so that they can, in fact, be productive interactions that develop the ethical competence of professors of educational administration and the students with whom they work.

Notes

1. Throughout the discussion of syllabi, we note the number of courses exhibiting a certain theme or pattern. At times a single syllabus

contained points that caused us to classify it as demonstrating more than one theme. Similarly, some contained nothing to cause us to place it into a particular category. Thus the numbers do not "add up" to a fixed total.

2. For analyses of a similar line of activity in K-12 education, see Murphy (1990a, 1991a, 1992b).

5

Laying a Foundation for
Dialogues on Ethics: A Proposal

*The most striking feature of contemporary moral utterance is that
so much of it is used to express disagreements; and the most striking
feature of the debates in which these disagreements are expressed is
their interminable character.*

Alasdair MacIntyre from *After Virtue*
(1981), p. 6

Disagreement and diversity in ethics beget worries.

Jeffrey Stout from *Ethics After Babel* (1988),
p. 13

A central tenet of this volume is that in recent years, discussions about
educational ethics have increased in number and expanded in scope.
Once hesitant to consider the importance of nonquantifiable entities
such as "values" or "moral commitments," academics and practitioners
alike are beginning to recognize that education is "invested from the
outset with a moral character" (Hodgkinson, 1991, p. 26) and that those
wishing to understand and work effectively in this field must reckon
with its ethical dimensions. This acknowledgement does not, however,
guarantee that discussions of educational ethics will proceed in a
smooth or productive manner. Indeed, topics related to values and to
moral commitments (or standards) for students, educators, or their
families tend to provoke interactions that lead to one of three outcomes.
When discussions begin with references to "popular" ethics—those
linked to caring, justice, equity, quality, and the like—participants

quickly profess their shared commitments and then go on to use these ethics to justify a widely disparate set of policies and practices.[1] At other times, when the merit of specific plans or actions is the focus, proponents of a particular policy or strategy impugn the moral integrity of those holding opposing views.[2]   And, under some circumstances, persons who are frustrated by the fact that "there seems to be no rational way of securing moral agreement in our culture" (MacIntyre, 1981, p. 6) abandon serious consideration of their own or others' ethical stances and decide that "any moral system not guilty of self-contradiction is as good as any other" (Stout, 1988, p. 14).

All of these outcomes are, in some way, less than ideal. In the first situation, self-reflection upon the meaning of ethical commitments is neglected. In the second, opportunities for growth and increased understanding are often lost. The third condition, in turn, tends to discourage a spirit of critique capable of "uncovering inherent injustice or dehumanization imbedded in the language and structures of society" (Starratt, 1991, p. 189).

Scholars who have considered these alternative results of discussions of morality have offered a number of recommendations regarding productive ethical discourse. MacIntyre (1981), for example, argues that disagreements over ethics are "unsettlable ... [and that] our society cannot hope to achieve moral consensus" (p. 235). He therefore calls for "the construction of local forms of community" (p. 245) within which individuals, sharing similar values and assumptions, discover ways "intellectual and moral life can be sustained" (p. 245). For MacIntyre, enclaves of like-minded persons provide the only milieu for sustained and satisfying conversations about ethics. James Q. Wilson (1993), in contrast, offers evidence for the existence of an innate "natural moral sense ... [that] shapes human behavior and the judgments people make of the behavior of others" (p. 2). He calls for the nurturance of this sense and argues that persons who do so will uncover ways to live more humanely and to discuss their deepest beliefs and values. Others—such as Richard Rorty (1989)—deny the existence of any "core self" (p. 189) and of moral truth that is "out there" (p. 27) and argue for the acceptance of the need for personal creations of meaning and for the simultaneous pragmatic acceptance of the need to discover ways individuals engaged in the private processes of "self-creation" (p. 43) can learn to live together.

In spite of their differences, MacIntyre (1981), Wilson (1993), and

Rorty (1989) agree on the importance of discourse on ethics. For them, as authors and philosophers (at least in a broad sense), such discourse seems to be a fairly effortless process. For those of us in educational administration who are not as comfortable trafficking in the language of values and morals, it is likely to be a more arduous procedure— especially so when we interact with others who may not share our understandings and assumptions. It is for those in this latter group that this chapter is written. We tackle the assignment of enhancing discourse by presenting a framework for thinking about key underpinnings of assertions about "good" and "bad," "right" and "wrong."

Before we begin, three points are worthy of note. First, we wish to stress that the decision to concentrate upon the "underpinnings" of ethical commitments was a deliberate one, made for the following reason. As we analyzed the three typical outcomes of ethical discussions noted above—hasty superficial agreement, hostility and closedmindedness, and acceptance of a completely relativistic stance— we concluded that, all too often, participants in such discussions fail to understand their own or others' underlying assumptions about human nature, society, and the ways ethics can, do, or should influence interactions. Discussants treat these presuppositions as universal "givens" and assume that everyone is operating under roughly the same beliefs. Then, instead of understanding that alternative views may be entirely "logical" if one is operating under a different set of assumptions and beliefs,[3] they become angry or frustrated when others differ in their conclusions. Thus it would seem that productive dialogues about ethical commitments must *begin* with an understanding of beliefs, assumptions, and expectations. We therefore offer a framework for thinking about these foundational presuppositions.

Second, the goal is to provide a conceptual framework that colleagues can use in at least three ways: (1) to help us think deeply and critically about our own personal and professional beliefs and commitments; (2) to increase our ability to understand the moral reasonings of others, to respect their values even when we do not agree with them, and to continue to engage in dialogue on these important topics; and (3) to provide some of the foundations for the inclusion of ethics in administrator preparation programs.

A third and final point relates to the scope and comprehensiveness of this chapter. This framework is not intended to present an exhaustive list of the categories of assumptions that underlie and inspire moral beliefs and practices. Rather, it highlights several important issues that, in the view of scholars who have probed the process and products of moral reasoning, are inextricably linked to ethical commitments. Issues to be examined include:

1. Actual, perceived, and desired conceptions of purposes—in this instance, of education's purposes
2. Beliefs about human nature
3. Understandings of actual and ideal communities
4. Perceptions of value, the nature of commitments to pursue them, and the role of ethics in helping persons honor those commitments
5. Epistemological assumptions regarding the nature of "truth" and "reality," legitimate types of knowledge, and strategies for inquiry and discovery
6. Attitudes toward moral tensions, ambiguities, uncertainties, and paradoxes

In the sections that follow, we examine each of these topics, noting scholarship that emphasizes the links between undergirding beliefs and ethical commitments.

Conceptions of Purpose

Discussions about the purposes of education often focus upon the instrumental goals of schools (Foster, 1986). The central concern is with identifying standards that can focus the energies of educators and provide yardsticks against which their work can be measured. Such a conception of purpose, although not necessarily incorrect, is limited. It does not raise questions about the basis for choosing some standards over others, about the ways measurements of success or failure will be used, and other fundamental issues. Indeed, in linking education's purposes to the achievement of short-term, measurable goals, this conception fails to reckon with the pervasiveness and power of profound (but perhaps unconscious) beliefs about purpose to influence thinking about the morality of attitudes, actions, policies, and practices.

Hodgkinson (1991) discusses the links between notions of purpose and commitments to values when he writes:

All human organizations, whether they are simple or complex, exist to achieve purposes. These purposes in turn are rooted in human desires or values. Each organization seeks to serve its members and its clientele by altering the world in such a way as to realize those values. (p. 26)

Hodgkinson suggests that many educational leaders fail to consider the values that they and their schools honor and promote. In accepting prevailing cultural norms, they have drifted into assumptions about education's purpose. This, in turn, has led to ethical commitments (e.g., competitive ethics) that emphasize enhancing individual students' chances to achieve "success"—defined quantitatively and comparatively. All too often, these ethics ignore the ways schools can and should "establish and enhance the values of security, health, the common good, the interest of the state, the capacity for profit, wealth of all sorts and the highest values of philosophy, ideology, and religion" (p. 27). Hodgkinson challenges educational leaders—and, we would add, those persons who educate them—to reflect upon this constellation of purposes and embrace ethical stances that honor them and the persons affected by them.

Hodgkinson is not alone in asserting that conceptions of purpose are distinct from and foundational to goals and that they need to be examined because of their ethical implications. By examining and critiquing assumptions regarding purpose, Bellah et al. in *The Good Society* (1991) challenge the idea that "educational and occupational systems . . . have an objective givenness that puts them beyond question" (p. 43). They are especially critical of "the notion of education as a means for the acquisition of wealth" (p. 169). Noting that this idea "leaves the basic structure of the educational institution unexamined while it claims to be responding to the already fixed 'preferences' students bring with them" (p. 170), Bellah et al. suggest that this idea of purpose can lead to ethics and practices that are fundamentally inhumane. Contending that educators must recognize and eschew views of education that threaten to harm persons in *any* way, they call, instead, for a focus on education as "life enabling" (p. 176). When this is acknowledged as a worthy aim, Bellah and his colleagues argue that we can begin to develop schools that nurture and support individuals and their communities in ways that dignify persons and the cultures and groups to which they belong.

In a similar vein, Joel Spring (1985) asserts that beliefs about the purposes of public schools must be examined by educators, policymakers, and concerned citizens. He offers discussions of three categories of purpose—political, social, and economic—and argues that all have been operative in the decisions about educational organization, leadership, curricula, pedagogies, and standards. In Spring's view, these decisions have moral implications in that they influence the treatment of individuals and groups and the types of values to be supported or undermined in our society. He argues that serious reflection upon this topic must focus, not only on the actual and espoused purposes, but also on the forces that cause us to favor certain purposes (or certain versions of these purposes) over others.

Beliefs About Human Nature

In addition to delving into conceptions of purpose, those wishing to promote dialogues about ethics in schooling might wish to examine individual and institutional understandings of human nature. Within education, some attention has been paid to this topic. However, scholarship often attempts to isolate, examine, and manipulate only selected human characteristics. When human nature is considered from a more holistic, philosophical/ethical perspective, discussions about the nature of persons have other emphases. One focus might involve understanding views of women and men as agents capable of willfully making commitments and acting upon them. Another might require considering conceptions of persons as independent individuals, participants in intimate and casual friendship and familial relationships, and as members of local communities and national and global societies.

Greenfield (1984, 1991) argues that persons are "acting, willing, passionate, fearful, hoping, moral, fallible individuals" (1984, p. 152). He further contends that organizations are nothing more than the constructions of these individuals. For Greenfield, any effort to understand an educational organization (or, for that matter, any organization) as an entity is grounded in faulty assumptions. Schools must be understood in terms of the individuals who inhabit them. Furthermore, he suggests that individuals must be understood as persons whose wills, thoughts, interpretations, and intentional activities are grounded in beliefs about values and about moral and immoral ways to pursue and honor those values.

John Macmurray (1957, 1961; see also Dokecki, 1990; Kirkpatrick, 1986) is another who argues that ethical commitments are linked to assumptions about human nature. Noting the existence of a *"crisis of the personal,* the Western intellectual tradition's lack of a practical and meaningful understanding of the person" (Dokecki, p. 158, emphasis in the original, commenting on Macmurray's work), he questions two aspects of Western thought: the tendency to emphasize the rational and define persons principally as thinkers and a penchant for viewing persons as isolated individuals. For Macmurray these two trends have resulted in inaccurate, ethically bankrupt perspectives on persons and their interactions. In *The Self as Agent* (1957), he suggests that persons are fundamentally actors, doers, agents (*agere,* to act), not reason-driven thinkers. In *Persons in Relation* (1961), he asserts that relationships are ontological realities and that interdependent interactions, not isolation, characterize personhood. Macmurray argues that we must attend to these two perspectives if we are to understand the practical and ethical nature of persons and their formal and informal interactions and if, as scholars, we are to develop the appropriate strategies for examining moral dimensions of organizational life.

Both Greenfield (1984, 1991) and Macmurray (1957, 1961) explicitly articulate their views of the nature of humans and discuss links between these and certain assumptions about personal and organizational morality. Equally instructive might be a consideration of implicit assumptions, both our own and others', as they are revealed in preferred policies and practices and in the links between these assumptions and our ethical commitments. For example, persons holding the view that we are fundamentally individuals who come together in social systems to further our own, private interests are likely to maintain that contractual and competitive ethics are needed to govern human interactions (e.g., Gilder, 1981; Hobbes, 1651/1962; Nozick, 1974; Rawls, 1971). It is entirely possible that such persons would gravitate toward a meritocratic notion of schooling—one in which competition is encouraged, individual achievement rewarded and personal failures attributed to a lack of will or effort. Further, those embracing this perspective may assume that individuals who do not succeed will be motivated by their lack of rewards and by the observation of others enjoying the fruit of their labor (Levin, 1992). In contrast, those who assume that we are inherently social in nature would, in all likelihood, gravitate toward ethics that encourage cooperation and caring (e.g., Beck, 1992, 1994a;

Buber, 1958, 1965; Gilligan, 1982; Noddings, 1984, 1989, 1992). These scholars would, it seems, prefer organizational structures that provide multiple opportunities for students, teachers, parents, and others to work together (see e.g., Beane, 1990), and pedagogical strategies such as cooperative learning (Slavin, 1983) would exemplify processes that support shared efforts. Personal success would not figure as prominently in the value systems of those holding this view, and, when it was recognized, it would probably be linked to participation in group activities, not to individual effort or ability.

Understandings of Actual and Ideal Communities

Even as beliefs about the nature of persons influence ethical perspectives, so also do understandings of actual and ideal communities, for one of the functions of ethics is governing interactions so that persons can live together well.[4] Notions of what living together does and should mean would, therefore, shape concepts of morality even as ethical perspectives would shape ideas and ideals of community.

Frank Kirkpatrick in *Community: A Trinity of Models* (1986) offers a helpful analysis of the reciprocal relationship between beliefs about community and ethics. He argues that at least three models have dominated Western thought and have shaped beliefs about preferred social and individual ethics. Kirkpatrick describes the first model as "atomistic/contractarian" (p. 13). This model, which revolves around the belief that communities are gatherings of self-interested individuals who come together because, in so doing, they can best further their private interests, has been quite influential in the United States. He suggests that, within this model, an ethic of competition governed by certain social contracts, is looked to as a principal moral guide.

Kirkpatrick's second model contrasts sharply with his first. In the "organic/functional" model, community is similar to an organism that has as an "underlying characteristic . . . its totality" (p. 65). "[As such] it is to be taken as a unified whole which is not simply the sum of its parts but is itself a basic unity comprising and in an interdependent relationship with its parts" (p. 63). Those who hold to this as an ideal of community are likely to look to ethics emphasizing cooperation, perhaps even compliance, unselfishness, and sacrifice as primary guides for human interaction.

Kirkpatrick labels his third model as "mutual/personal" (p. 137).

Within this model, neither individuals nor the social collective as an organic unity takes precedence over the other. Rather, this perspective assumes that persons are ontologically relational and that communities characterized by interdependence and mutuality support personal development. In this ecological model, the well-being of persons and the well-being of communities are linked, and efforts to nurture individuals must also nurture those inhabiting the social networks that provide the milieux for growth and healthy development.

Kirkpatrick's models are general descriptions of types of human networks or collective gatherings. It is possible, however, to find specific examples of each of these types in education and see how a preference for a particular model of community might shape the ethics toward which school leaders gravitate. The first model, which assumes that persons are essentially isolated individuals who come together chiefly to increase personal chances for success or happiness, has been, it would seem, the one which has exerted the most influence on educational policy and practice. Much of what happens in both K-12 and higher education is aimed at encouraging and rewarding individual achievement and discouraging group activities. Indeed, the essential organization of the classroom bears witness to this reality, for as Goodlad (1984) notes, in most classes, "each student essentially works and achieves alone within a group setting. A class may be praised for its performance, but this recognition, more often than not, is for the sum or average of individual performances, not some shared, collaborative accomplishment" (p. 123). In such classes, an ethic of competition would almost inevitably hold sway over one of caring and cooperation.

Perceptions of Value

Attributions of value clearly comprise an important part of the subset of assumptions that influence ethical commitments. Identifying these "concepts of the desirable" (Hodgkinson, 1991, p. 89) is therefore an important step in understanding the forces driving moral beliefs and activities arising from them. Overt expressions can provide clues to the notions of value held by persons, cultures, and groups. These, however, can also be misleading because professed values often differ rather dramatically from actual ones. Fortunately, other indicators of value preferences exist and are accessible to persons trying to understand educational belief systems. An analysis of organizational and decision-making structures can provide clues to administrative values. Pedagogical practices, in turn, reveal attitudes about the substance, purposes, and processes of teaching and learning. In a similar way, rules, policies, and procedures provide clues to the relative values placed upon order, creativity, obedience, equity, efficiency, caring, and the like. And, as Bolman and Deal (1990, 1991) ably document, symbols in the form of legends, logos, metaphors, ceremonies, and such are powerful revealers of the values landscape.

Identifying values is important but not by itself sufficient to provide an adequate understanding of the ways values influence ethics. Gaining this kind of understanding demands an exploration of value hierarchies—a phrase we use to refer to preferences, beliefs, and priorities that lead individuals and organizations to view some moral commitments as fundamental and nonnegotiable; others as preferable; others as optional; and still others as unacceptable. In his discussion of the moral nature of educational leadership, Hodgkinson (1991) presents his views on ethical hierarchies. In a chapter titled "Value Theory," he first discusses values (and their related ethics) that compete for influence over the thoughts and actions of organizational leaders and their followers. Hodgkinson offers a model wherein values exist on a continuum, ranging from "the axiological (good) [to the] deontological (right). The former refers to what is enjoyable, likable, pleasurable: the latter to what is proper, 'moral,' duty bound, or simply what *ought* to be" (p. 97). Discussing this model, Hodgkinson offers three postulates. One of these relates to the existence of a hierarchy. He suggests that deontological, right values "are superior, more authentic, better justified, of more defensive grounding" (p. 103) than those linked to the satisfaction of a preference or the pursuit of pleasure. He also suggests that organizations and their leaders tend to avoid dealing with genuinely moral (i.e., right) values (which require some "act of faith or commitment" [p. 99]) preferring instead to deal with those that are more "affective, idiosyncratic, idiographic, . . . direct, . . . basically asocial and hedonistic" (p. 99). Anyone attempting to understand the ethos of an educational organization might benefit greatly by looking at the strength of commitments of various participants to the types of values within Hodgkinson's schema.

A similar view has been offered by critical theorists and feminist scholars.[5] As a group, they have contributed much to our understanding of ways in which assumed and accepted values such as those linked to "competition, hyperachievement, and . . . excellence" (Giroux, 1988, p. 27) have subtly and not so subtly served to undermine "creative, self-transforming, life-transforming morality" (Giroux, 1988, p. 37). Like Hodgkinson, they suggest that education's potential to help all persons grow, develop, and participate in shaping their own destiny has been blunted by unquestioning acceptance of prevailing norms. It is the contention of this group of scholars that an examination of the deep value structures of organizations and cultures will lead to a recognition of the ways "the dominant culture so actively conceals and precludes whenever possible" (Giroux, 1988, p. 37) just and compassionate educational endeavors.

Hodgkinson (1991) and Giroux (1988) imply that an ongoing critique of values and a continuing commitment to pursue the finest of these will change education, moving it toward becoming an increasingly noble endeavor. In asserting this, they are making certain assumptions about the ways value-driven ethics affect human life. In essence, they are suggesting that the ideal role of educational ethics is a transformative one—that ethics should function to shape perceptions and understandings so that persons view themselves, others, and circumstances in ways that promote good, right, or just ends. Those who share this view would therefore expect moral commitments to have a dramatic effect upon those who hold them. They would find it difficult to separate personal and professional ethics and would expect all areas of a person's life to reflect his or her deepest beliefs and values.

This is a very legitimate way to understand the role of ethics and values in our lives. It is not, however, the only way. Others (see e.g., Beauchamp & Childress, 1984; Crittenden, 1984; Kultgen, 1988), although not denying the potential of ethics to transform lives, underscore the fact that moral principles and value-based commitments can be quite useful to educators and other professionals who must make decisions in difficult, problematic circumstances. Arguing that "human beings are moral agents . . . responsible for their choices and [possessing] a duty to make choices in morally responsible ways" (Strike, Haller, & Soltis, 1988, p. 6), individuals holding this view tend to emphasize that an awareness of ethical principles is especially useful when one confronts dilemmas. Moral principles can provide assistance in reasoning and choosing from among alternatives. Those within this camp would not, necessarily, expect a commitment to certain values to entail a significant change in a person's sense of self and others. Rather they would look to these values to provide logical rationales for action in the midst of difficult circumstances.

Epistemological Assumptions

The acceptance of certain values and their attendant ethics depends, in part, upon epistemological assumptions, for consciously held beliefs depend, at least in part, upon assumptions about truth, reality, and knowledge. Considerable evidence (see e.g., Campbell et al., 1987; Culbertson, 1988) indicates that positivistic assumptions about reality, truth, and legitimate knowledge have held sway in school administration. These have led to an infatuation with efficiency and productivity (Callahan, 1962; Toch, 1991) and a tendency to emphasize ethics of competition and utility that seem most likely to ensure that excellence is attained in an efficient manner (Beck, 1992, 1994a; Shea, 1991). In recent years, these values and ethics—and their epistemological infrastructure—have been called into question by numerous scholars who believe positivism cannot help in answering questions dealing with virtue, justice, caring, compassion, and how educational leaders do and should grapple with these and other values. T. B. Greenfield, a leading member of this group, argues that organizational reality consists of ever-changing, individual realities—realities emerging from an admixture of facts, beliefs, hopes, passions, needs, and desires. He states that "the established empiricist highroad to truth, objectivity, and control in social organizations" (1991, p. 2) is in reality "a delusionist dream, a nightmare . . . that needs exorcism to liberate and restore the human and moral perspective" (p. 2). As an alternative, he recommends learning to know, via a dialectical dialogue, an ongoing endeavor in which persons engage in "a continuing process of discovery aimed at gaining an understanding of ourselves and others—a process aimed at understanding social reality and its artifacts which we call organizations" (1988, p. 109).

Like Greenfield, Foster (1986) suggests that positivistic approaches—used in isolation—are inadequate for comprehending persons or organizations, and, for this reason, they are unable to provide guidance for developing ethics capable of informing and improving individual and corporate life. In his view, at least part of the superficial morality and ethical pathology evident in so many educational settings is linked to a naive acceptance of traditional epistemological assumptions. Citing

Morgan (1980, see also 1986), Foster (1986) posits that beliefs about what constitutes legitimate knowledge "govern the dominant metaphors" (p. 57) of an organization. While helping to shape scholarship, policy, structures, and practices, these metaphors also influence and reflect beliefs about the kinds of institutions schools should be and the types of activities school leaders should pursue. Therefore, assumptions about the nature and pursuit of knowledge are linked to ethics. A solid comprehension of the latter requires an understanding of the former.

Echoing many of the ideas offered by Greenfield (1991) and Foster (1986), Mark Johnson, in *Moral Imagination* (1993), describes a kind of knowing that he believes is essential for the development of morality capable of influencing "the complex, evolving, and imaginative character of actual human meaning, cognition, and reason" (pp. 123-124). Arguing that "conceptualization and reasoning are largely imaginative" (p. 259), Johnson sets forth a "theory of imaginative rationality" (p. 125). He argues that an engagement with human experiences as revealed through art and through narrative descriptions can engender "a deep, reflective knowledge of the metaphorical [i.e., imaginative] nature of human understanding and of the metaphors that structure one's own moral understanding" and that this knowledge is foundational to living and acting morally.

The impact of assumptions about knowledge and knowing upon educational ethics has been discussed articulately by Thomas Sergiovanni in *Moral Leadership* (1992). Drawing upon the work of Hunter Lewis (1990), he describes six modes of knowing that influence values. "'Some value systems are based on authority; others are based on deductive logic, sense experience, emotion, intuition, or science'" (p. 11, quoting Lewis, p. 12). Sergiovanni notes that educational decisions and policies—moral and otherwise—have, in recent years, been based most often upon deductive logic and science and that, for this reason, these ways of knowing have generally been trusted to produce authentic, legitimate, sound insights. He, however, contends that "in recent years, sense experience and intuition have made important inroads into legitimacy as modes of knowing" (p. 14). He welcomes this trend, arguing that the acceptance of multiple ways of knowing will assist educators in moving beyond technique and developing a sense of moral craft in their work.

Noddings (1984, 1992) goes even further than Sergiovanni in calling for the acceptance of multiple ways of knowing. Focusing especially on the types of knowledge we seek to develop in students, she asserts that many educational efforts are morally bankrupt because they focus on cognition and fail to reckon with "the existential heart of life—one that draws attention to our passions, attitudes, connections, concerns, and experienced realities" (1992, p. 47). For Noddings, this requires that educators embrace a kind of knowing that emphasizes "skills, attitudes, and capacities traditionally associated with women" (1992, p. xiii; see also Chodorow, 1978; Gilligan, 1982; Ruddick, 1980, 1989). Her discussions of the differences between educational programs that embrace relational knowledge and an ethic of caring and those that do not provide helpful examples of the ways epistemological assumptions influence educational practices, their related values, and moral commitments.

Attitudes Toward Ambiguities

The choices individuals or groups make regarding legitimate types of knowledge and ways of knowing are linked, in part, to attitudes toward complex, puzzling, or ambiguous situations and concepts. Analyses of historical trends suggest that persons with a low tolerance for uncertainty are attracted to understandings of reality that emphasize objectivity, sensory knowledge that yields measurable results, and the possibility of discovering final "correct" answers to educational questions (Beck & Murphy, 1993; Culbertson, 1988; Foster, 1986). In all likelihood, they would gravitate toward an understanding of ethics as a rationally derived set of problem-solving principles that, properly applied, can untangle dilemmas and simplify complex situations so that the best, or the right, solution or course of action can be found (Hauerwas & Burrell, 1977). Ethics of competition and utility would be especially appealing for persons with this view, for both look to measurable results to guide decisions about right and wrong.

In educational arenas, many policymakers, administrators, teachers, and students seem to be especially interested in avoiding ambiguity.[6] Looking to quantified data, they apparently consider strategies that produce high scores for the most people at the lowest cost to be both practically and morally right. Indeed, for many it seems that no important distinctions exist between practicality, efficiency, economy, productivity, and morality. For those who accept this way of thinking, ambiguous, uncertain, nonmeasurable dimensions of schools often are dismissed or ignored. They, in the words of Hauerwas and Burrell (1977), believe that "the 'personal' can only be morally significant to the extent that it can be translated into the 'impersonal'" (p. 18).

Johnson (1993) argues that this tendency to run from ambiguity has, historically, sparked the development of an elaborate system of moral absolutes. He claims that these elaborate systems have tended to fall into one of two categories. Some (e.g., Kantianism) tend to "excessive abstractionism" (p. 120) in which the uniqueness of each person and situation is obliterated by a concern with discovering universal ethical principles, applicable to all persons and all situations at all times (see also Taylor, 1982). Others (e.g., utilitarianism) tend to "reductionism" in that they strive to determine the moral rightness or wrongness of an act solely on the basis of its ability to increase the good—measured in some way and defined by that measure—for the greatest number of persons. In Johnson's view this results in a kind of "moral arithmetic . . . [wherein one engages in] acts of adding and averaging what is taken to be an objectively quantifiable good, commodity, or property of an object or situation" (p. 121). Johnson argues that this ignores the wonder and greatness of human life.

Johnson (1993) calls upon persons "to never be fooled into thinking that our [moral] formalizations can stand for our embodied, ongoing, historically situated, and imaginative moral experience" (p. 260). Writing years earlier, Miklos (1977-1978) issues a similar call especially to educational administrators. Indeed, he suggests that anyone working in this field must wrestle with a host of moral dilemmas. For example, the school leader must consider the extent to which she or he should engage in manipulative practices by controlling communication and the flow of information in her or his institution. Closely related to this, an administrator must also decide if and when deception (which could be achieved simply by withholding of certain bits of information) is justified. Additionally, Miklos also argues that school leaders must struggle with competing loyalties and with desires to serve (and please) various constituencies and that they must wrestle with multiple interests and concerns as they attempt to cultivate a particular type of climate or culture in schools. For Miklos, those who attempt to simplify these situations by disregarding the puzzles and ambiguities deny the true nature of educational leadership. As he admonishes scholars and practitioners to recognize the uncertainties inherent in their profession, he further challenges them to consider moral responses to them.

Several authors have offered actual and hypothetical descriptions of educators who have accepted the inevitability of ambiguity with a special eye to the moral commitments of these persons. Noddings (1992), at length, describes her alternative vision of schools in which caring for persons and accepting their inconsistencies and complexities take precedence over a concern with a specific, circumscribed body of knowledge or set of principles. Sergiovanni (1991), similarly, describes educational leaders who are able to live with and balance competing ethical impulses. In turn, Beck (1994b) describes a principal who helped to transform a troubled urban high school into a caring community of learners. One of the notable characteristics of this leader was her ability to accept the fact that many of her decisions would not have clear-cut, "right" solutions. Beck suggests that this principal's ability to accept her own fallibility and lack of omniscience enabled her to accept and enjoy the "humanness" of others and encourage a spirit of acceptance in her school.

Concluding Thoughts

As departments of educational administration engage in efforts to address ethical issues in their programs, they face several challenges. Professors must wrestle with personal and institutional understandings of moral leadership. Further, they must assess their responsibility to teach prospective school executives to think and act ethically. And they must consider the pedagogical strategies that will enable them to honor their responsibilities in this area. As we have noted throughout this volume, many faculty members are beginning to undertake these tasks.

This development is, in our view, an exciting and important one. As we have asserted here and elsewhere, the first goal of preparation programs should be to help students articulate an explicit set of values and beliefs to guide their actions—to become moral agents (Beck & Murphy, 1993) or what C. Hodgkinson (1975) calls "valuationists" (p. 16). This goal, it seems, is being considered in many of our institutions and, in some, has been accepted as one worthy of attention and effort.

Even as we applaud movements in this direction, we also, however, feel a certain wariness. The history of preparation efforts, in many ways, is a story of efforts to provide administrators with principles and procedures for simplifying and controlling the ambiguities they inevitably encounter. It is also a chronicle of repeated failures of such approaches to produce leaders able to grapple with the complex realities of life in schools. If we reduce ethics to a set of techniques that we must discover and transmit, we run the risk of repeating this pattern. One way to avoid this is to enlarge our discussions of approaches to this topic. In addition to discussing course content, teaching strategies, assessment, and like topics, we might also engage in dialogue about the issues highlighted in this chapter. For, in our view, preparing administrators for ethical practice requires more than the establishment of courses. It demands that faculty and students engage in ongoing reflection and conversation about their beliefs and commitments and the ways in which practices and policies support or contradict these. In this chapter, we offer a framework for the kind of self-examination and dialogue that can ensure that efforts to address ethics in preparation programs resist the tyranny of technique and, instead, promote moral thinking and acting in departments of educational administration and in our schools.

Notes

1. The history of schooling provides numerous examples of this phenomenon. For example, one would be hard-pressed to find a time in the past century when leaders in America's schools *did not* assert their commitments to certain fundamental tenets of democracy such as the equality and worth of all persons. These same leaders, however, supported (and at times instituted) policies and practices that resulted in highly unequal, often demeaning treatment of various groups and persons.

2. Recent discussions of outcome-based education (Harp, 1993) and of standards and expectations for students and teachers (Bradley, 1993) of homosexuals provide vivid examples of discussions with ethical overtones that become verbal (if not literal) battlegrounds.

3. Numerous examples of situations where persons, not understanding their own or others' underlying beliefs, failed to engage in constructive dialogue might be given. For example, David Elkind, in *The Hurried Child: Growing Up Too Fast Too Soon* (1981) describes a number of incidents where persons blithely engaged in developmentally destructive practices because they did not consider their beliefs

about the nature of childhood and healthy development. He tells, for instance, of parents who declare their unconditional acceptance and love, but who act in ways that suggest children must earn these things by performing and achieving. Implicit in Elkind's work is the idea that conscious examination of deeply held assumptions and expectations has the potential to enable persons to order their actions in a manner more consistent with these beliefs and commitments.

4. Clearly these are links between one's beliefs about human nature and assumptions about the kinds of communities that are right and appropriate for persons possessing such nature. We, however, have chosen to discuss these in separate sections. An understanding of our assumptions about both would, it seems, be useful in helping us thoughtfully consider issues in educational ethics. Assumptions about the nature of persons might especially influence thinking about inter-personal morality. Beliefs about community, in turn, would probably shape our thinking about the ethics of certain organizational practices and structures.

5. Even beginning to name persons in these groups is a daunting task. Some whose work has been especially influential in identifying links between underlying norms and beliefs and educational policies and practices include Apple (1982), Aronowitz and Giroux (1985), Foster (1986), McLaren (1991), Noddings (1984, 1992), and Shakeshaft (1987).

6. For examples of this tendency in policy arenas, see Kirp's (1989) discussion of the concerns of some state, district, and local administra-tors when they were forced to make decisions about the admission and treatment of youngsters with AIDS in public schools. Vinovskis's (1988) work on the political processes surrounding the issue of adolescent pregnancy also demonstrates that government officials tend to search for "facts" in the form of quantifiable data to help them find clear, unambiguous solutions to complex problems.

Afterword

There is now a wide resurgence of interest in the teaching of ethics in the preparation of educational administrators. This has been due, I think, to a recognition in the social sciences generally of the limits of the scientific paradigm for investigating and discovering regularities in the human condition, a recognition of the value of narrative and qualitative inquiry in contributing to our understanding of "what's going on here," and a recognition that human actions are ultimately guided by some framework of values. This volume contributes to this literature by explicitly examining how moral philosophy has been embraced in the preparation of educational administrators in research-oriented universities.

The authors have done the following, and have done it well.

They have provided a historical review of ethics in administration, showing how the field has moved from the "philosophical-statesman" ethos of an earlier era to a mimicry of science and an emphasis on technique, with a concomitant decline in interest in the inclusion of morals and philosophy in preparation programs.

They have demonstrated how changes in the social landscape have affected educational administration, and how, as a result, there has been a resurgence of interest in ethics and values. Indeed, if nothing else, our last several decades of United States politics have been lessons in ethics: from Eisenhower's warning regarding the military-industrial complex, to Nixon's fall from grace, to our current scandals of public office. All of this, of course, jumps into public consciousness, and from there drifts into questions about schools and their administration. Public officials, including school administrators, become accountable and responsible, and ethics and values become terms of significance.

Beck and Murphy have described and analyzed the current scene in educational administration. They have cataloged and analyzed the state of the teaching of ethics in UCEA institutions. One of their findings of considerable interest is that many approaches to including ethics in the curriculum adopt a problem-solving or decision-making agenda, often using cases and examples. A second finding is that much attention is paid to the analysis or development of professional, and sometimes personal, codes of ethics.

Beck and Murphy have argued that the ethics curriculum can basically be divided into three areas—courses that stress knowledge about ethics and ethical systems, issue-oriented courses, and those courses that offer some combination.

This suggests to me that much that is done with ethics and moral philosophy in preparation programs reflects to a substantial degree what I might call dilemma ethics. That is, ethics is seen as a set of moral dilemmas to which there is often no satisfactory solution. The resolution of the dilemma is then analyzed under a rule-ethic formula: If we apply the rule of utilitarianism, what results? How does Kantian universalism apply? What would Rawls say? and so on, with perhaps the ultimate question at the end: What would you do?

Rule ethics and dilemma resolution as modes for introducing ethical reasoning are fine avenues, but in my view they represent, as the sociologists say, necessary but not sufficient variables. Indeed, in one way of looking at this, the irresolvable nature of moral argument in this society—from the dissension around the big issues of equality and liberty, efficiency and effectiveness, justice and compassion, to the daily critical moral incidents of our lives—suggests the fragmentation and dissolution of all major ethical theories and systems.

It seems that many decisions ultimately are made without foundation, arbitrarily, and are justified more by preference than by right. That is why there is such a close tie between ethics courses and legal issues. The law at least gives us a platform upon which to justify the decision. But on what is the law based? Were the segregationist and misogynist laws of our recent past based on anything other than preference? Surely not on the right and just. Then how do we know that we too are not caught unwittingly in a time of injustice?

This is where, I think, rule ethics must give way to a consideration of virtue ethics, an ethics that asks the fundamental question, "How do we wish to live?" Rather than seeing ethics as individual problem solving, we might ask what virtues, what character, do we need? How do we build *communities of character*? This, I think, is the ultimate administrative question. It would be to our good, then, and to the good of administrative preparation, that a virtue ethics, an ethics not of dilemmas but of character, be stressed.

That is why I found the last section of the book so encouraging. There the authors have shown the more recent emphasis on the building of character encouraging reflection and learning from the drama of the humanities. I hope this trend continues. If our preparation programs continue to examine the character and nature of the essence of administration, then there is hope not only for our schools, but for our world.

William P. Foster
Indiana University

Afterword

The authors have done the field a service in providing a clear overview of the history and present practice of attempts at ethical education for prospective and practicing administrators I see this study as a necessary first step for a series of follow-up studies of this important topic. I believe some of those studies should be case studies of individual graduate courses, which would explore the narrative of the professor as well as the narratives of the students before, during, and after the courses.

We know precious little about how professors balance the academic ideal of rigorous scholarship with what might be called the more pastoral concern to nurture and challenge the ethical values and worldviews of their students. Furthermore, we know precious little about the attitudes, beliefs, or personal journeys of the educators practicing in administrator preparation programs. One assumes that their biographies reveal family influences, positive and negative role models, the painful disillusionment of childhood idealism, and pragmatic responses to politically threatening dilemmas as they advanced in their careers. It would be interesting to study in detail how the diverse personalities in the class, already shaped by diverse personal histories, respond to the content of the course. That response can go in two directions. It can lead to a deepening reflection on one's personal ethical choices; it can also lead to a deepening reflection on the larger ethic of the institution we call schooling. In the happiest result, it will lead to both. But what that means in each individual case will be different both in depth and in content.

I could go on in this vein, suggesting many specific research studies that this book might stimulate, but I will leave that to the imaginations of the authors and others for whom this topic holds similar fascination. Instead I'd like to turn to a discussion of two observations the authors make in their fourth chapter. One concerns the identification by some participants in the study of a basic justification for taking up the ethical education of school administrators; namely, that leadership involves significant influence over people's lives and that there is therefore a need to develop a sensitivity to the moral aspects of that influence both in terms of the way the influence is exerted and in what people are being influenced to do. The second concerns the practice of some of the participants in the study of exposing their students to ethical dilemmas that have no easy or clear solution, but simply a variety of solutions depending on the point of view of the respondent.

It is true that leaders exercise influence over people's lives. At this point, I am not so much interested in exploring what this influence is (e.g., to get them to try a whole language approach, or to get parents to volunteer to serve on project teams) as in where the power to exert such influence comes from. Leaders, in contrast to bureaucrats, get people to try things, change, move into something new, expand their perspectives. Besides the clarity of thinking, which enables others to grasp what it is they are being encouraged to try, leaders exert a morally compelling force, something that persuades others to believe that what they are being encouraged to try is a moral good. Manuals and guidebooks, for example, can logically outline how a teacher can work out a computer-assisted social studies class. The manual does not, however, give the teacher a morally compelling reason—one that speaks to the good of the student (and of society)—to use this powerful tool to explore public policy options that are embedded in a particular historical case. But an educator whose moral sense is attuned to the importance of developing in students the skills of democratic debate over public policy may seize upon a sophisticated computer simulation of, say, the writers of the constitution debating a particular article, as a good tool to stimulate such a debate. Besides being a tool to advance understanding of what took place historically, the educator sees this simulation as a means to achieve a moral good—namely, the nurturing of democratic discussion. When that educator goes to other teachers in the school to persuade them to try this approach, he or she is clearly seeking to influence the lives of other people.

This simple example can stand for many other instances of influence that leaders exert on people's lives. The moral force behind that influence, as it may be nurtured in a graduate course on ethics, comes from something much deeper. It will be found in the narrative of that person's life—in the influences of parents, role models, and heroes; in the lessons learned from a multitude of positive as well as painful experiences; from reflecton on the commentaries of historians, poets, and novelists. Such moral force comes from a life of trying to make sense out of experience, of asking how life should be lived, of exploring utopias and infernos. In short, the moral force of leadership comes from a lifetime's search for meaning and purpose in human existence. It is this deeper search that I want to highlight, for the literature on leadership tends to deal with behaviors or skills and competencies and is silent about the deeper quest that fuels and energizes leadership. Research needs to probe the complexities, ambiguities, and depth of such a life search. I suspect we will find a much richer tapestry of moral development in the lives of administrators than in the logical deduction of Kantian moral imperatives. Such research will also caution those who would treat the ethical implication of leadership to avoid the trap of what I call the quick fix. Their courses must somehow tap into the deeper journey of their students if they are to have a lasting impact.

My second comment concerns the laudable practice of exposing graduate students to ethical problems that appear to have many or sometimes no solutions. In many instances, the response to a situation—for example, a fight in the school yard—can vary depending on the cognitive or cultural map one uses to interpret what happened, on the basic stance one takes about how one educates morally, and toward what vision of the moral life one wishes to point his or her students. The interpretation can involve a simplistic appraisal of what school rules were violated and therefore what predetermined sanctions are called for. The interpretation can involve an understanding of ethnic- and class-shaped responses to insults, and the response might move toward bringing about a mutual understanding between the combatants. The interpretation might involve a perspective on the tendency toward violence in young males, and the response may be a lesson in nonviolent resolutions of conflict. By exposing graduate students to these various interpretations and responses, professors help to broaden the ethical perspectives their students bring to their work.

But there are some situations for which there are no satisfying solutions—situations like rape and child abuse and character assassination and many other examples of mean-spirited and destructive actions. Ethical education also needs to confront the tragic quality of human life. Humans act irrationally, senselessly, foolishly, childishly, selfishly—causing irreparable harm to one another. We need to confront those destructive tendencies, for they are the cause of so much tragedy in the human experience. We have yet to find a way to transform these tendencies in humans so that they disappear, remain dormant, or are channelled into positive acts that contribute to rather than destroy life.

Hence, the only ethical response to some situations is to weep, extend sympathy and support to those in pain, and feel compassion toward the person whose life is so mixed up and filled with fear and rage that he or she is compelled to hurt and destroy. Besides the virtues of justice and care, then, we need to teach the virtue of compassion. Perhaps the best response to the fight in the school yard should be one grounded in compassion, a deep understanding that we have inside of us—all of us—a capacity to wound and hurt. Adults have perfected that capacity in much more subtle ways, but the violation of other persons, however minor and only partially intended, is a constant in human life. And it is tragic that we engage in it. Based on compassion for the young people in the school yard, who are simply responding as they have been socialized to act, educators might not only use this school yard occasion to teach the combatants the values of caring, but also recognize the need to recreate the whole environment of the school, so that any form of fighting will be seen as a violation of another person, and so the value of caring and community will become the primary value in the school. We are not fated for a life of tragedy. We drift into it because we do not expend the energy and risk the vulnerability that caring requires. A strong community of caring individuals does not happen automatically and when it is momentarily achieved, it easily evanesces. In one sense the realization of a caring community is always in front of us waiting to be achieved. Community is a journey, not a destination—a journey with many potential dead ends, a journey through difficult and threatening terrain. Yet it can also be a journey of satisfying discovery, where, as C. S. Lewis put it so well, we are often "surprised by joy."

Robert J. Starratt
Fordham University

References

Achilles, C. M. (1988). Unlocking some mysteries of administration and administrator preparation: A reflective prospect. In D. E. Griffiths, R. T. Stout, and P. B. Forsyth (Eds.), *Leaders for America's Schools* (pp. 41-67). Berkeley, CA: McCutchan.

Alkire, G. (1978). Master's programs in educational administration. In P. F. Silver & D. W. Spuck (Eds.), *Preparatory programs for educational administration* (pp. 52-82). Columbus: University Council for Educational Administration.

Apple, M. (1982). *Education and power.* Boston: Ark.

Aronowitz, S., & Giroux, H. (1985). *Education under siege: The conservative, liberal and radical debate over schooling.* New York: Bergin & Garvey.

Astin, H. S., & Leland, C. (1991). *Women of influence, women of vision: A cross-generational study of leaders and social change.* San Francisco: Jossey-Bass.

Astuto, T. A. (1990). *Reinventing school leadership* (pp. 2-5) [Working memo prepared for the Reinventing School Leadership Conference]. Cambridge, MA: National Center for Educational Leadership.

Barnett, B. G., McQuarrie, F. O., & Norris, C. J. (Eds.). (1992). *The moral imperatives of leadership: A focus on human decency.* Fairfax, VA: National Policy Board for Educational Administration.

Barth, R. (1990). *Improving schools from within: Teachers, parents, and principals can make the difference.* San Francisco: Jossey-Bass.

Beane, J. A. (1990). Affective dimensions of effective middle schools. *Educational Horizons,* pp. 109-112.

Beauchamp, T. L., & Childress, J. F. (1984). Morality, ethics, and ethical theories. In P. A. Sola (Ed.), *Ethics, education and administrative decisions: A book of readings* (pp. 39-67). New York: Peter Lang.

Beck, L. G. (1992). Meeting future challenges: The place of a caring ethic in educational administration. *American Journal of Education, 100*(3), 254-296.

Beck, L. G. (1994a). *Reclaiming educational administration as a caring profession.* New York: Teachers College Press.

Beck, L. G. (1994b). Cultivating a caring school community: One principal's story. In J. Murphy & K. S. Louis (Eds.), *Reshaping the principalship* (pp. 177-202). Thousand Oaks, CA: Sage.

Beck, L. G., & Murphy, J. (1993). *Understanding the principalship: Metaphorical themes 1920s to 1990s.* New York: Teachers College Press.

Beck, L. G., & Newman, R. L. (1992, October). *Caring in contexts of diversity: Notes from the field.* Paper presented at the annual conference, University Council for Educational Administration, Milwaukee, WI.

Bellah, R. M., Madsen, R., Sullivan, W. M., Swidler, A., & Tipton, S. M. (1985). *Habits of the heart: Individualism and commitment in American life.* New York: Harper & Row.

Bellah, R. M., Madsen, R., Sullivan, W. M., Swidler, A., & Tipton, S. M. (1991). *The good society.* New York: Alfred A. Knopf.

Block, P. (1993). *Stewardship: Choosing service over self-interest.* San Francisco: Berret-Koehler.

Blum, L. (1991). Moral perception and particularity. *Ethics, 101,* 701-725.

Bok, D. C. (1982). *Beyond the ivory tower: Social responsibilities of the modern university.* Cambridge, MA: Harvard University Press.

Bolin, F. S. (1989, Fall). Empowering leadership. *Teachers College Record, 91*(1), 81-96.

Bolman, L., & Deal, T. (1990). *Modern approaches to understanding and managing organizations.* San Francisco: Jossey-Bass.

Bolman, L., & Deal, T. (1991). *Reframing organizations: Artistry, choice, and leadership.* San Francisco: Jossey-Bass.

Bradley, A. (1993, September 15). Not making the grade: Teachers firing spurs debate over standards, expectations for students. *Education Week, 13*(2), 1, 19-21.

Bridges, E. M. (1977). The nature of leadership. In L. L. Cunningham, W. G. Hack, & R. O. Nystrand (Eds.), *Educational administration: The developing decades* (pp. 202-230). Berkeley, CA: McCutchan.

Bridges, E. M., & Hallinger, P. (1991, Fall). Problem-based learning: A promising approach for preparing educational administrators. *UCEA Review, 32*(3), 2-5, 7-8.

Brieschke, P. A. (1990). The administrator in fiction: Using the novel to teach educational administration. *Educational Administration Quarterly, 26*(4), 376-393.

Brown, J. S., Collins, A., & Duguid, P. (1989). Situated cognition and the culture of learning. *Educational Researcher, 18*(1), 32-42.

Brown v. Board of Education of Topeka, 347 U.S. 483 (1954).

Buber, M. (1958). *I and thou* (2nd ed.). (R. Smith, Trans.). New York: Charles Scribner's Sons.

Buber, M. (1965). *Between man and man*. New York: Macmillan.

Bull, B. L. (1993). Ethics in the preservice curriculum. In K. A. Strike & P. L. Ternasky (Eds.), *Ethics for professionals in education: Perspectives for preparation and practice* (pp. 69-83). New York: Teachers College Press.

Button, H. W. (1966). Doctrines of administration: A brief history. *Educational Administration Quarterly, 2*(3), 216-224.

Callahan, D. (1980). Goals in the teaching of ethics. In D. Callahan & S. Bok (Eds.), *Ethics teaching in higher education* (pp. 61-80). New York: Plenum.

Callahan, D., & Bok, S. (1980). Hastings Center Project on the Teaching of Ethics: Summary recommendations. In D. Callahan & S. Bok (Eds.), *Ethics teaching in higher education* (pp. 299-302). New York: Plenum.

Callahan, J. C. (Ed.). (1988). *Ethical issues in professional life*. New York: Oxford University Press.

Callahan, R. E. (1962). *Education and the cult of efficiency*. Chicago: University of Chicago Press.

Callahan, R. E., & Button, H. W. (1964). Historical change of the role of the man in the organization: 1865-1950. In D. E. Griffiths (Ed.), *Behavioral science in educational administration* (Sixty-third NSSE yearbook, Part II, pp. 73-92). Chicago: University of Chicago Press.

Camenisch, P. F. (1983). *Grounding professional ethics in pluralistic society*. New York: Haven.

Campbell, R. F. (1981). The professorship in educational administration: A personal view. *Educational Administration Quarterly, 17*(1), 1-24.

Campbell, R. F., Fleming, T., Newell, L. J., & Bennion, J. W. (1987). *A history of thought and practice in educational administration*. New York: Teachers College Press.

Carnegie Council on Adolescent Development (1989). *Turning points*. Washington, DC: Author.

Chodorow, N. (1978). *The reproduction of mothering*. Berkeley: University of California Press.

Clark, C. M. (1990). The teacher and the taught: Moral transactions in the classroom. In J. Goodlad, R. Soder, & K. A. Strike (Eds.), *The *moral dimensions of teaching,* (pp. 251-265). San Francisco: Jossey-Bass.

Clark, D. L., & Meloy, J. M. (1989). Renouncing bureaucracy: A democratic structure for leadership in schools. In T. J. Sergiovanni & J. H. Moore (Eds.), *Schooling for tomorrow: Directing reforms to issues that count* (pp. 272-294). Boston: Allyn Bacon.

Cohen, D. K. (1976). Loss as a theme in social policy. *Harvard Educational Review, 46,* 553-571.

Cooper, B. S., & Boyd, W. L. (1987). The evolution of training for school administrators. In J. Murphy & P. Hallinger (Eds.), *Approaches to administrative training* (pp. 3-27). Albany: State University of New York Press.

Crittenden, B. (1984). The moral context of decision making in education. In P. A. Sola (Ed.), *Ethics, values, and administrative decisions: A book of readings* (pp. 15-38). New York: Peter Lang.

Cuban, L. (1992). Managing dilemmas while building professional communities. *Educational Researcher, 21*(1), 4-11.

Culbertson, J. A. (1964). The preparation of administrators. In D. E. Griffiths (Ed.), *Behavioral science in educational administration* (Sixty-third NSSE yearbook, Part II, pp. 303-330). Chicago: University of Chicago Press.

Culbertson, J. A. (1965). Trends and issues in the development of a science of administration. In Center for the Advanced Study of Educational Administration, *Perspectives on educational administration and the behavioral sciences* (pp. 3-22). Eugene: University of Oregon, Center for the Advanced Study of Educational Administration.

Culbertson, J. A. (1988). A century's quest for a knowledge base. In N. Boyan (Ed.), *Handbook of research on educational administration* (pp. 3-26). New York: Longman.

Culbertson, J. A., & Farquhar, R. H. (1970). Preparing educational leaders: Recruiting and selecting candidates from administrative preparation. *UCEA Newsletter, 12*(1), 10-13.

De Pree, M. (1989). *Leadership is an art.* New York: Doubleday.

Dewey, J. (1916). *Democracy and education.* New York: Macmillan.

Dewey, J. (1938). *Experience and education.* New York: Macmillan.

Dewey, J. (1963). *The school and society* (20th ed.). Chicago: University of Chicago Press.

Dokecki, P. (1990). On knowing the person as agent in caring relations. *Person-Centered Review, 5*(2), 155-169.

Durkheim, E. (1957). *Professional ethics and civic morals.* (C. Brookfield Trans.). London: Routledge & Kegan Paul. (Original Work published in 1950)

Eaker, D. J., & Van Galen, J. A. (1993). Introduction: Caring across educational boundaries. *The Urban Review: Issues and Ideas in Public Education, 25*(1), 1-4.

Elkind, D. (1981). *The hurried child: Growing up too fast, too soon.* Reading, MA: Addison-Wesley.

Erlandson, D. A., & Witters-Churchill, L. (1988, March). *Design of the Texas NASSP study.* Paper presented at the annual convention of the National Association of Secondary School Principals.

Evers, C. W. (1992). Ethics and ethical leadership: A pragmatic and holistic approach. In P. A. Duignan & R. J. S. MacPherson (Eds.), *Educative leadership* (pp. 21-43). London: Falmer Press.

Farquhar, R. H. (1968, October). The humanities and educational administration: Rationales and recommendations. *Journal of Educational Administration, 6*(2), 97-115.

Farquhar, R. H. (1981, June). Preparing educational administrators for ethical practice. *The Alberta Journal of Educational Research, 27*(2), 192-204.

Farquhar, R. H., & Piele, P. K. (1972). *Preparing educational leaders: A review of recent literature.* Danville, IL: Interstate. (ERIC/CEM state-of-the-knowledge series, No. 14, UCEA monograph series, No. 1)

Fenstermacher, G. D. (1990). Some moral considerations on teaching as a profession. In J. Goodlad, R. Soder, & K. A. Sirotnik (Eds.), *The moral dimensions of teaching* (pp. 87-129). San Francisco: Jossey-Bass.

Flanigan, J. L., & Richardson, M. D. (1992, April). *Analyses of educational administration programs in doctoral granting institutions.* Paper prepared for the annual meeting of the Society of Professors of Education, San Francisco.

Foster, W. (1984). The changing administrator: Developing managerial praxis. In P. A. Sola (Ed.), *Ethics, education and administrative decisions: A book of readings* (pp. 103-121). New York: Peter Lang.

Foster, W. (1986). *Paradigms and promises: New approaches to educational administration.* Buffalo, NY: Prometheus.

Foster, W. P. (1989, April). *School leaders as transformative intellectuals.* Paper presented at the American Educational Research Association, San Francisco, CA.

Fust, M. (1989). *The story of my wife: The reminiscences of Captain Stoerr* (I. Sanders, Trans.). London: Cape. (Original work published in 1957)

Gastil, R. D. (1977). *Social humanities.* San Francisco: Jossey-Bass.

Gilder, G. (1981). *Wealth and poverty.* New York: Basic Books.

Gilligan, C. (1982). *In a different voice: Psychological theory and women's development.* Cambridge, MA: Harvard University Press.

Giroux, H. A. (1988). *Schooling and the struggle for public life: Critical pedagogy in the modern age.* Minneapolis: University of Minnesota Press.

Good, T. L., & Marshall, S. (1984). Do students learn more in heterogeneous or homogeneous groups? In P. L. Peterson, L. C. Wilkinson, & M. Hallinan (Eds.), *The social context of instruction: Group organization and group processes* (pp. 15-38). Orlando, FL: Academic Press.

Goodlad, J. (1984). *A place called school.* New York: McGraw-Hill.

Goodlad, J. I., Soder, R., & Sirotnik, K. A. (Eds.). (1990). *The moral dimensions of teaching.* San Francisco: Jossey-Bass.

Grant, G. (1993). Discovering how you really teach. In K. A. Strike & L. P. Ternasky (Eds.), *Ethics for professionals in education: Perspectives for preparation and practice* (pp. 135-147). New York: Teachers College Press.

Greenfield, T. B. (1979). Organization theory as ideology. *Curriculum Inquiry, 9*(2), 97-112.

Greenfield, T. B. (1984). Leaders and schools: Willfulness and nonnatural order in organizations. In T. J. Sergiovanni & J. E. Corbally (Eds.), *Leadership and organizational culture: New perspectives on administrative theory and practice.* Urbana: University of Illinois Press.

Greenfield, T. B. (1988). The decline and fall of science in educational administration. In D. E. Griffiths, R. T. Stout, & P. B. Forsyth (Eds.), *Leaders for America's schools* (pp. 131-159). Berkeley: McCutchan.

Greenfield, T. B. (1991, April). Re-forming and re-valuing educational administration: Whence and when cometh the phoenix. *Organizational Theory Dialogue,* 1-16.

Greenfield, W. (1987). Moral imagination and interpersonal competence: Antecedents to instructional leadership. In W. Greenfield (Ed.), *Instructional leadership: Concepts, issues, and controversies* (pp. 56-73). Boston: Allyn & Bacon.

Greenleaf, R. K. (1977). *Servant leadership: A journey into the nature of legitimate power and greatness.* New York: Paulist Press.

Gregg, R. T. (1960). Administration. In C. W. Harris (Ed.), *Encyclopedia of educational research* (3rd ed., pp. 19-24). New York: Macmillan.

Gregg, R. T. (1969). Preparation of administrators. In R. L. Ebel (Ed.), *Encyclopedia of educational research* (4th ed., pp. 993-1004). London: MacMillan.

Griffiths, D. E. (1959). *Administrative theory.* New York: Appleton-Century-Crofts.

Griffiths, D. E. (1988). *Educational administration: Reform PDQ or RIP* (Occasional paper, no. 8312). Tempe, AZ: University Council for Educational Administration.

Griffiths, D. E., Stout, R. T., & Forsyth, P. B. (Eds.). (1988). *Leaders for America's Schools.* Berkeley, CA: McCutchan.

Gross, J. (1993). The legal context of professional ethics: Values, standards, and justice in judging teacher conduct. In K. A. Strike & P. L. Ternasky (Eds.), *Ethics for professionals in education: Perspectives for preparation and practice* (pp. 202-216). New York: Teachers College Press.

Hall, R. M., & McIntyre, K. E. (1957). The student personnel program. In R. F. Campbell & R. T. Gregg (Eds.), *Administrative behavior in education* (pp. 393-425). New York: Harper.

Hallinger, P., Leithwood, K., & Murphy, J. (Eds.). (1993). *Cognitive perspectives on educational leadership.* New York: Teachers College Press.

Halpin, A. W. (1960). Ways of knowing. In R. F. Campbell & J. M. Lipham (Eds.), *Administrative theory as a guide to action* (pp. 3-20). Chicago: University of Chicago, Midwest Administration Center.

Hampel, J. (1988). *The administrator as servant: A model for leadership development.* Unpublished manuscript, Department of Education, San Diego State University.

Harlow, J. G. (1962). Purpose-defining: The central function of the school administrator. In J. A. Culbertson & S. P. Hencley (Eds.), *Preparing administrators: New perspectives* (pp. 61-71). Columbus, OH: University Council for Educational Administration.

Harp, L. (1993, September 22). PA parent becomes mother of 'outcomes' revolt. *Education Week, 13*(3), 1, 19-21.

Hauerwas, S., & Burrell, D. (1977). From system to story: An alternative pattern for rationality in ethics. In S. Hauerwas (Au.), *Truthfulness and tragedy: Further investigations into Christian ethics.* Notre Dame, IN: University of Notre Dame Press.

Heller, A. (1985). The basic question of moral philosophy. *Philosophy and Social Criticism, 1*(11), 57-59.

Hills, J. (1978). Problems in the production and utilization of knowledge in educational administration. *Educational Administration Quarterly, 14*(1), 2.

Hobbes, T. (1962). *Leviathan, or the matter, forme and power of a commonwealth ecclesiasticall and civil.* New York: Collier. (Original work published in 1651)

Hodgkinson, C. (1975, Winter). Philosophy, politics and planning: An extended rationale for synthesis. *Educational Administration Quarterly, 11*(1), 11-20.

Hodgkinson, C. (1991). *Educational leadership: The moral art.* Albany: State University of New York Press.

Immegart, G. L., & Burroughs, J. M. (Eds.) (1970). *Ethics and the school administrator.* Danville, IL: Interstate.

Ishiguro, K. (1989). *The remains of the day.* New York: Knopf.

Jackson, P. W., Boostrom, R. E., & Hansen, D. T. (1993). *The moral life of schools.* San Francisco: Jossey-Bass.

Johnson, M. (1993). *The moral imagination: Implications of cognitive science for ethics.* Chicago: University of Chicago Press.

Kerchner, C. T. (1988, November). Bureaucratic entrepreneurship: The implication of choice for school administration. *Educational Administration Quarterly, 24*(4), 381-391.

Kirby, P. C., Paradise, L. V., & Protti, R. (1992). Ethical reasoning of educational administrators: Structuring inquiry around the problems of practice. *Journal of Educational Administration, 30*(4), 25-32.

Kirkpatrick, F. G. (1986). *Community: A trinity of models.* Washington, DC: Georgetown University Press.

Kirp, D. (1989). *Learning by heart: AIDS and school children in America's communities.* New Brunswick, NJ: Rutgers University Press.

Kirst, M. W., McLaughlin, M., & Massell, D. (1989). *Rethinking children's policy: Implications for educational administration.* Stanford, CA: Stanford University, Center for Educational Research at Stanford.

Kluger, R. (1977). *Simple justice.* New York: Vintage.

Knowles, M. S. (1990). *The adult learner: A neglected species.* Houston: Gulf.

Koestenbaum, P. (1987). *The heart of business: Ethics, power, and philosophy.* Dallas: Saybrook.

Koestenbaum, P. (1991). *Leadership: The inner side of greatness.* San Francisco: Jossey-Bass.

Kozol, J. (1991). *Savage inequalities: Children in America's schools.* New York: Crown.

Kultgen, J. (1988). *Ethics and professionalism.* Philadelphia: University of Pennsylvania Press.

Levin, H. (February, 1992). *Accelerated Schools.* Presentation to the faculty, Graduate School of Education, University of California, Los Angeles.

Levine, S. L., Barth, R. S., & Haskins, K. W. (1987). The Harvard principals' center: School leaders as adult learners. In J. Murphy & P. Hallinger (Eds.), *Approaches to administrative training* (pp. 150-163). Albany: SUNY Press.

Lewis, H. A. (1990). *Question of values.* New York: Harper Collins.

MacIntyre, A. (1966). *A short history of ethics.* New York: Macmillan.

MacIntyre, A. (1981). *After virtue: A study in moral theory.* Notre Dame, IN: University of Notre Dame Press.

Macmillan, C. J. B. (1993). Ethics and teacher professionalization. In K. A. Strike & P. L. Ternasky (Eds.), *Ethics for professionals in education: Perspectives for preparation and practice* (pp. 189-201). New York: Teachers College Press.

Macmurray, J. (1957).*The self as agent.* London: Faber.

Macmurray, J. (1961). *Persons in relation.* New York: Harper & Bros.

Mann, D. (1975). What peculiarities in educational administration make it difficult to profess: An essay. *Journal of Educational Administration, 12*(1), 139-147.

March, J. G. (1978, February). American public school administration: A short analysis. *School Review, 86,* 217-250.

May, W. F. (1980). Professional ethics: Setting, terrain, and teacher. In D. Callahan & S. Bok (Eds.), *Ethics teaching in higher education* (pp. 205-241). New York: Plenum.

McCarthy, M. M., Kuh, G. D., Newell, L. J., & Iacona, C. M. (1988). *Under scrutiny: The educational administration professorate.* Tempe, AZ: University Council for Educational Administration.

McLaren, P. (1991). Critical pedagogy: Constructing an arch of social dreaming and a doorway of hope. *Journal of Education, 173*(1), 9-34.

Miklos, E. (1977-78). Ethical aspects of administrative action: Implications for research and preparation. *Administrator's Notebook, 26*(5), 1-4.

Miklos, E. (1990). Ministrative insight: Educational administration as pedagogic practice: An essay review of Philip Rodney Evan's dissertation. *Phenomenology and Pedagogy, 8,* 337-342.

Miklos, E., & Nixon, M. (1978). *Educational administration programs in Canadian universities.* Edmonton, Canada: The University of Alberta, Department of Educational Administration.

Miller, J. B. (1986). *Toward a new psychology of women.* Boston: Beacon.

Milstein, M. M., & Associates (1993). *Changing the way we prepare educational leaders: The Danforth experience.* Newbury Park, CA: Corwin Press.

Mitchell, B. (1990a). Loss, belonging, and becoming: Social policy themes for children and schools. In B. Mitchell and L. Cunningham (Eds.), *Educational leadership and changing contexts in families, communities, and schools: Eighty-ninth yearbook of the National Society for the Study of Education* (pp. 19-51). Chicago: University of Chicago Press.

Mitchell, B. (1990b). Children, youth, and restructured schools: Views from the field. In B. Mitchell and L. Cunningham (Eds.), *Educational leadership and changing contexts in families, communities, and schools: Eighty-ninth yearbook of the National Society for the Study of Education* (pp. 52-68). Chicago: University of Chicago Press.

Morgan, G. (1980). Paradigms, metaphors, and puzzle solving in organization theory. *Administrative Science Quarterly, 26,* 605-622.

Morgan, G. (1986). *Images of organization.* Newbury Park, CA: Sage.

Mulkeen, T. A., & Tetenbaum, T. J. (1990). Teaching and learning in knowledge organizations: Implications for the preparation of school administrators. *Journal of Educational Administration, 28*(3), 14-22.

Murdoch, I. (1970). *The sovereignty of good.* London: Routledge & Kegan Paul.

Murphy, J. (1989, October). *The place of the dissertation in professional programs of study in educational administration.* Panel presentation at the annual conference of the University Council for Educational Administration, Scottsdale, AZ.

Murphy, J. (1990a). The reform of school administration: Pressures and calls for change. In J. Murphy (Ed.), *The reform of American public education in the 1980s: Perspectives and cases* (pp. 277-303). Berkeley, CA: McCutchan.

Murphy, J. (1990b). Preparing school administrators for the twenty-first century: The reform agenda. In B. Mitchell & L. L. Cunningham

(Eds.), *Educational leadership and changing contexts of families, communities, and schools: Eighty-ninth yearbook of the National Society for the Study of Education* (pp. 232-251). Chicago: University of Chicago Press.

Murphy, J. (1990c). Restructuring the technical core of preparation programs in educational administration. *UCEA Review, 31*(3), 4-5, 10-13.

Murphy, J. (1991a). *Restructuring schools: Capturing and assessing the phenomena.* New York: Teachers College Press.

Murphy, J. (1991b, Spring). The effects of the educational reform movement on departments of educational leadership. *Educational Evaluation and Policy Analysis, 13*(1), 49-65.

Murphy, J. (1992a). *The landscape of leadership preparation: Reframing the education of school administrators.* Newbury Park, CA: Corwin.

Murphy, J. (1992b). School effectiveness and school restructuring: Contributions to educational improvement. *School Effectiveness and School Improvement, 3*(2), 90-109.

Murphy, J. (1993a). Ferment in school administration: Rounds 1-3. In J. Murphy (Ed.), *Preparing tomorrow's school leaders: Alternative designs* (pp. 1-17). University Park, PA: University Council for Educational Administration.

Murphy, J. (1993b, May). Restructuring schooling: The equity infrastructure. *School Effectiveness and School Improvement, 4*(2), 111-130.

Murphy, J. (1993c). Alternative designs: New directions. In J. Murphy (Ed.), *Preparing tomorrow's school leaders: Alternative designs* (pp. 225-253). University Park, PA: University Council for Educational Administration.

Murphy, J. (in press a). The knowledge base in educational administration: Historical footings and emerging trends. In R. Donmoyer & J. Scheurich (Eds.), *The knowledge base in educational administration: Multiple perspectives.* Albany: State University of New York Press.

Murphy, J. (in press b). Administrative preparation: Preservice. In P. T. Husen & T. N. Postlethwaite (Eds.), *The International Encyclopedia of Education* (2nd edition). Oxford: Pergamon.

Murphy, J. (in press c). The changing role of the superintendency in restructuring districts in Kentucky. *School Effectiveness and School Improvement.*

Murphy, J., & Hallinger, P. (1987). Emerging views of the professional

development of school administrators: A synthesis with suggestions for improvement. In J. Murphy & P. Hallinger (Eds.), *Approaches to administrative training* (pp. 245-281). Albany: State University of New York Press.

Murphy, J., & Hallinger, P. (1989, March-April). Equity as access to
learning: Curricular and instructional treatment differences. *Journal of Curriculum Studies, 21*(2), 129-149.

Murphy, J., & Hallinger, P. (1992). The principalship in an era of
transformation. *Journal of Educational Administration, 30*(2), 77-88.

Murphy, J., & Louis, K. S. (Eds.) (1994). *Reshaping the principalship:
Lessons from transformative reform efforts.* Thousand Oaks, CA:
Corwin.

Muth, R. (1989, October). *Reconceptualizing training for educational administrators and leaders: Focus on inquiry* (Notes on Reform, no. 2).
Charlottesville, VA: National Policy Board for Educational Administration.

National Association of Elementary School Principals. (1990). *Principals
for the 21st century schools.* Alexandria, VA: Author.

National Commission for the Principalship. (1990). *Principals for our
changing schools: Preparation and certification.* Fairfax, VA: Author.

National Policy Board for Education Administration (1989, May). *Improving the preparation of school administrators: The reform agenda.*
Charlottesville, VA: Author.

Newlon, J. H. (1934). *Educational administration as social policy.* New
York: Scribner.

Noddings, N. (1984). *Caring: A feminine approach to ethics and moral
education.* Berkeley: University of California Press.

Noddings, N. (1988a). An ethic of caring and its implications for instructional arrangements. *American Journal of Education, 96*(3), 215-230.

Noddings, N. (1988b). Educating moral people. In M. Brabeck (Ed.),
*Who cares: Theory, research, and educational implications of the ethic of
care* (pp. 216-232). New York: Praeger.

Noddings, N. (1989). Educating moral people. In M. Brabeck (Ed.), *Who
cares: Theory, research and ethical implications of the ethic of care.* New
York: Praeger.

Noddings, N. (1992). *The challenge to care in schools.* New York: Teachers
College Press.

Noddings, N. (1993). Caring: A feminist perspective. In K. A. Strike &
P. L. Ternasky (Eds.), *Ethics for professionals in education: Perspective*

for preparation and practice (pp. 43-53). New York: Teachers College Press.

Norton, M. S., & Levan, F. D. (1987, Winter). Doctoral studies of students in educational administration programs in UCEA member institutions. *Educational Considerations, 14*(1), 21-24.

Nozick, R. (1974). *Anarchy, state, and utopia.* New York: Basic Books.

Oakes, J. (1985). *Keeping track: How schools structure inequality.* New Haven, CT: Yale University Press.

Ortiz, F. I., & Marshall, C. (1988). Women in educational administration. In N. Boyan (Ed.), *Handbook of research on educational administration* (pp. 123-142). New York: Longman.

Osterman, K. F., & Kottkamp, R. B. (1993). *Reflective practice for educators: Improving schooling through professional development.* Newbury Park, CA: Corwin.

Peterson, P. (1993). Facing up. *The Atlantic, 272*(4), 77-90.

Pincoffs, E. (1971). Quandary ethics. *Mind, 80,* 552-571.

Pitner, N. (1987). Hormones and harems: Are the activities of superintending different for a woman? In P. A. Schmuck, W. W. Charters, & R. O. Carlson (Eds.), *Educational policy and management sex differentials* (pp. 273-295). New York: Academic Press.

Plato (1976). *Protagorus.* (C. C. W. Taylor, Trans.). Oxford: Clarendon.

Pohland, P. A., & Carlson, L. T. (1993, Fall). Program reform in educational administration. *UCEA Review, 34*(3), 4-9.

Popper, S. H. (1990). *Pathways to the humanities in school administration* (3rd ed.). Tempe, AZ: University Council for Educational Administration.

Prestine, N. A., & LeGrand, B. (1990, April). *Cognitive learning theory and the preparation of educational administrators: Implications for practice and policy.* Paper presented at the annual meeting of the American Educational Research Association, Boston, MA.

Purpel, D. (1989). *The moral and spiritual crisis in education: A curriculum for justice and compassion in education.* New York: Bergin & Gervey.

Quality Education for Minorities Project. (1990). *Education that works: An action plan for the education of minorities.* Cambridge, MA: Harvard University Press.

Rawls, J. (1971). *A theory of justice.* Cambridge, MA: Harvard University Press.

Rorty, R. (1982). *Consequences of pragmatism: Essays, 1972-1980.* Minneapolis: University of Minnesota Press.

Rorty, R. (1989). *Contingency, irony, and solidarity*. Cambridge: Cambridge University Press.

Ruddick, S. (1980). Maternal thinking. *Feminist Studies, 6*(2), 342-367.

Ruddick, S. (1989). *Maternal thinking: Towards a politics of peace*. Boston: Beacon.

Sarason, S. B. (1990). *The predictable failure of educational reform*. San Francisco: Jossey-Bass.

Schmuck, P. A. (Ed.). (1987). *Women educators: Employees of schools in western countries*. Albany, NY: State University of New York Press.

Schon, D. A. (1983). *The reflective practitioner: How professionals think in action*. New York: Basic Books.

Schon, D. A. (1987). *Educating the reflective practitioner*. San Francisco: Jossey-Bass.

Scott, M., & Rothman, H. (1992). *Companies with a conscience: Intimate portraits of twelve firms that make a difference*. New York: Birch Lane.

Sergiovanni, T. J. (1980, Winter). A social humanities view of educational policy and administration. *Educational Administration Quarterly, 16*(1), 1-19.

Sergiovanni, T. J. (1984). Developing a relevant theory of administration. In T. J. Sergiovanni & J. E. Corbally (Eds.), *Leadership and organizational culture: New perspectives on administrative theory and practice* (pp. 275-291). Urbana, IL: University of Illinois Press.

Sergiovanni, T. J. (1987). *The principalship: A reflective practice perspective* (1st ed.). Boston: Allyn & Bacon.

Sergiovanni, T. J. (1989). Mystics, neats, and scruffies: Informing professional practice in educational administration. *The Journal of Educational Administration, 27*(2), 7-21.

Sergiovanni, T. J. (1991). The dark side of professionalism in educational administration. *Phi Delta Kappan, 72*(7), 521-526.

Sergiovanni, T. J. (1992). *Moral leadership: Getting to the heart of school improvement*. San Francisco: Jossey-Bass.

Sergiovanni, T. J. (1993a). *Organizations or communities? Changing the metaphor changes the theory*. Invited Address, American Educational Research Association annual meeting, Atlanta, GA.

Sergiovanni, T. J. (1993b). *Building community in schools*. San Francisco: Jossey-Bass.

Shakeshaft, C. (1987). *Women in educational administration*. Newbury Park, CA: Sage.

Shapiro, J. P., & Smith-Rosenberg, C. (1989). The "other voices" in contemporary ethical dilemmas: The value of the new scholarship on women in the teaching of ethics. *Women's Studies International Forum, 12*(2), 199-211.

Shea, C. (1991). Pentagon vs. multinational capitalism: The political economy of the 1980s school reform movement. In C. M. Shea, E. Kahane, & P. Sola (Eds.), *The new servants of power: A critique of the 1980s school reform movement* (pp. 3-38). New York: Praeger.

Sichel, B. (1993). Ethics committees and teacher ethics. In K. A. Strike & P. L. Ternasky (Eds.), *Ethics for professionals in education: Perspectives for preparation and practice* (pp. 162-175). New York: Teachers College Press.

Silver, P. F. (1978). Some areas of concern in administrator preparation. In P. F. Silver & D. W. Spuck (Eds.), *Preparatory programs for educational administrators in the United States* (pp. 202-215). Columbus, OH: University Council for Educational Administration.

Silver, P. F. (1982). Administrator preparation. In H. E. Mitzel (Ed.), *Encyclopedia of educational research* (5th ed., Vol. 1; pp. 49-59). New York: Free Press.

Silver, P. F., & Spuck, D. W. (Eds.). (1978). *Preparatory programs for educational administrators in the United States.* Columbus, OH: University Council for Educational Administration.

Slater, R. O. (1991, April). On some recent developments in educational administration. *Organizational Theory Dialogue, 1*, 18-21.

Slavin, R. E. (1983). *Cooperative learning.* New York: Longman.

Spring, J. (1985). *American education.* New York: Longman.

Starratt, R. J. (1991). Building an ethical school: A theory for practice in educational leadership. *Educational Administration Quarterly, 27*(2), 185-202.

Stout, J. (1988). *Ethics after Babel: The languages of morals and their discontents.* Boston: Beacon.

Strike, K. A. (1993). Teaching ethical reasoning using cases. In K. A. Strike & T. L. Ternasky (Eds.), *Ethics for professionals in education: Perspectives for preparation in practice* (pp. 102-116). New York: Teachers College Press.

Strike, K. A., Haller, E. J., & Soltis, J. F. (1988). *The ethics of school administration.* New York: Teachers College Press.

Strike, K. A., & Soltis, J. F. (1992). *The ethics of teaching.* New York: Teachers College Press.

Strike, K. A., & Ternasky, P. L. (Eds.). (1993). *Ethics for professionals in education: Perspectives for preparation and practice.* New York: Teachers College Press.

Taylor, C. (1982). The diversity of goods. In B. Williams & A. Sen (Eds.), *Utilitarianism and beyond* (pp. 129-144). Cambridge: Cambridge University Press.

Thomas, B. R. (1990). The school as a moral learning community. In J. Goodlad, R. Soder, & K. A. Sirotnik (Eds.), *The moral dimensions of teaching* (pp. 266-295). San Francisco: Jossey-Bass.

Toch, T. (1991). *In the name of excellence: The struggle to reform the nation's schools, why it's failing, and what should be done.* New York: Oxford University Press.

Tyack, D. B., & Hansot, E. (1982). *Managers of virtue: Public school leadership in America, 1920-1980.* New York: Basic Books.

Vaill, P. B. (1984). *The purposing of high performing systems.* In T. J. Sergiovanni & J. Corbally (Eds.), *Leadership and organizational culture: New perspectives on administrative theory and practice* (pp. 85-104). Urbana: University of Illinois Press.

Vinovskis, M. (1988). *An "epidemic" of adolescent pregnancy? Some historical and political considerations* New York: Oxford University Press.

Wagstaff, L. H., & Gallagher, K. S. (1990). Schools, families, and communities: Idealized images and new realities. In B. Mitchell & L. L. Cunningham (Eds.), *Educational leadership and changing contexts of families, communities, and schools* (Eighty-ninth NSSE yearbook, pp. 91-117). Chicago: University of Chicago Press.

Watson, B. C. (1977). Issues confronting educational administrators, 1954-1974. In L. L. Cunningham, W. G. Hack, & R. O. Nystrand (Eds.), *Educational administration: The developing decades* (pp. 67-94). Berkeley: McCutchan.

Weinstein, F. (1989). Health educators: Where are you? *Health Education, 19*(16), 21-22.

Weisbord, M. R. (1987). *Productive workplaces: Organizing and managing for dignity, meaning, and community.* San Francisco: Jossey-Bass.

Whitehead, A. M. (1933). *Adventures of ideas.* New York: Macmillan.

Willower, D. J. (1988). Synthesis and projection. In N. J. Boyan (Ed.), *Handbook of research on educational administration* (pp. 729-747). New York: Longman.

Wilson, J. Q. (1993). *The moral sense.* New York: The Free Press.

Wynn, R. (1972). *Unconventional methods and materials for preparing educational administrators.* Danville, IL: Interstate. (ERIC/CEM state-of-the-knowledge series, No. 15, UCEA monograph series, No. 2)